Kelly McEvenue trained with Frank Ottiwell at the American Center for the Alexander Technique, San Francisco. She has taught extensively in Canada, with the Stratford Festival Theatre Company and the Stratford Festival Conservatory for Classical Theatre Training. In Toronto, she has taught at the Soulpepper Theatre Company, Mirvish Productions (on *The Lion King*), the University of Toronto Opera School and the Ryerson Theatre School. Internationally, she has taught at the Guildhall School of Music and Drama, London; the Centre for Development and Graduate Training in the Alexander Technique, London; and the Interlochen School for Performing Arts, Michigan. Kelly has assisted Patsy Rodenburg in her workshops for voice teachers at Britain's Royal National Theatre. She has been a movement consultant for television and film. Kelly lives in Toronto, Ontario, with her photographer husband Michael Rafelson and daughter Molly.

To my parents,
one loved the 'literature on it' and one loved to move.

The Actor and the Alexander Technique

KELLY MCEVENUE

First published 2002 by
PALGRAVE MACMILLAN™
175 Fifth Avenue, New York, N.Y. 10010 and
Houndmills, Basingstoke, Hampshire, England RG21 6XS.
Companies and representatives throughout the world.

PALGRAVE MACMILLAN is the global academic imprint of the Palgrave Macmillan
division of St. Martin's Press, LLC and of Palgrave Macmillan Ltd.
Macmillan® is a registered trademark in the United States, United Kingdom and other countries. Palgrave is a registered trademark in the European Union and other countries.

ISBN 0-312-29515-4

Library of Congress Cataloging-in-Publication Data available from the Library of Congress.

First published in the United Kingdom in 2001 by Methuen Publishing Ltd

First palgrave macmillan edition: August 2002
10 9 8 7 6 5 4 3 2

Printed in the United States of America

Contents

Acknowledgements

I would never have written this book without a gauntlet being laid. My deep-felt thanks to Patsy Rodenburg, whose friendship has always presented me with challenges and opportunities. Thanks to Michael Earley who helped me with the conception of this book, to my editor David Salmo and to the staff at Methuen who helped me through to completion.

I wish to acknowledge the countless actors and students who have participated in my work, they are the heart and soul of this book. To the actors and theatre folk whose voices and experience were shared: Brian Bedford, Butch Blake, Martha Burns, Joyce Campion, Andrew Croft, June Crowley, Cynthia Dale, Diane D'Aquila, Marion Day, Megan Dunlop, Stephen Dow, Colm Feore, Jude Haines, Desmond Heeley, Rita Howell, William Hutt, Krista Jackson, Debra Johnson, Eleanor Johnston, Claire Jullien, Dirk Lombard, Roberta Maxwell, Seana McKenna, Stephen Ouimette, Lucy Peacock, Janine Pearson, Goldie Semple, Ian Watson, Judy White, Jamie Williams – I could not have written this book without your insight.

To my family, teachers and friends, who know exactly how they have supported me throughout my teaching years, and with this project: Marj Barstow, Nancy Brown, Roy Brown, Laura Burton, Serena Condello, David Gorman, Mimi McEvenue and Geoff Love, George and Debbie McEvenue, Sheilagh McEvenue, Kiloran McRae, Sandra Niman, Frank Ottiwell, Mary and Burke Seitz, John Wood, Meg and Greg Young.

I am most grateful for my two inspiring artists, who know me best and see me through everyday, thanks to my daughter Molly and my husband Michael Rafelson.

Foreword

Kelly McEvenue is one of the world's finest Alexander teachers and theatre coaches.

Kelly and I first met at the Stratford Festival Theatre, Ontario, Canada, in 1984. This began a creative working partnership that has grown over the years and constantly enhances my teaching. Kelly has spirit, enthusiasm and joy when she works. She always uses positive reinforcement to release actors, never negativity.

Back in 1984 Kelly and I were part of a large movement and voice team at the Festival Theatre. Every morning there was a compulsory company warm-up from 10.00 to 10.45 – up to 70 actors gathering to be worked-out by a movement coach, followed by a vocal workout taken by me. Kelly had not been contracted to take the movement warm-up but started to attend to watch the work.

Anyone who has ever coached in a large theatre company will be keenly aware that those companies always contain a contingent of actors who, for whatever reason, are not ambitious, not hungry to be good, changed or worked. They are content to 'swell a scene or two', speak a few lines. Acting is a mundane job to this breed. They are mostly men, mostly the heavy-drinking, heavy-smoking brigade. They are often cynical and don't really want to rehearse and they definitely don't want to attend a morning warm-up! In short, they are the coach's nightmare. It is easy to teach ambitious actors and students but this contingent is the real test.

Kelly and I were sitting watching in horror as the movement coach was losing control of the company warm-up. Actors were standing around chatting at the back of the rehearsal room, not working, not listening and the coach was close to tears. Suddenly, Kelly was on her feet. Her energy and engagement immediately focused the company.

'Come on guys,' she said 'let's warm up. Let's learn how to lean on a bar using the Alexander Technique.' They laughed and she had them working within minutes.

For me that was the first sign of Kelly's skills, but she also warmed them up in such a way that made my following voice session more efficient. We had begun to work in harmony.

All teachers want to work on their subject profoundly and organically but in large theatre companies coaches rarely get to work in this way. Many coaches end up despairing about restrictions placed on their work. Not Kelly. Her humour and flexibility is essential in a company. She does her work when and how she can without devaluating the Alexander Technique but aware that she can't be precious about it when a company's demands on an actor are so complex.

These demands – from directors, tight schedules and the nature of high-tech productions – can place an actor's body at risk. I know that Kelly's calm and realistic approach to her work has saved many actors' bodies and, consequently, their careers.

So it can go like this:

The rehearsed fight between 20 heavily armoured knights wielding enormous swords is relocated at the technical rehearsal on to a steep rake beside a 10-foot drop. The actors can hardly see through their visors, they are sliding on the rake, pulling their knees, back, shoulders and necks. They are furious and feel pressurised because the director is trying to finish the technical before the first public preview in the evening.

Enter Kelly. Without stopping the flow of the rehearsal she will make the fight safe. Make each individual centred and calm. Actors will laugh with Kelly, stop moaning. She will solve the problems yet maintain the artistic shape of the fight.

Kelly likes actors; she wants them to succeed and she constantly supports them. She never moans about actors or blames them when they don't come up to her standards. She just stays with them and supports them whenever they are in the process. That's why I love talking about the work with her. So many coaches ridicule actors which is always depressing, as we are there to enable the artist not to mock them.

This book is a great insight into Kelly's clear and essential work. For me this book will be a constant reminder of Kelly's qualities when the Atlantic Ocean divides us. Anyone interested in theatre, the actor's body and the process of training will find a wealth of insights and humanity in this book.

Patsy Rodenburg
August 2001

AN INTRODUCTION TO
The Actor and
the Alexander Technique

Introduction

◡

I truly love my job in the theatre. I am a certified teacher of the Alexander Technique. For over eighteen years, I have been teaching the Alexander Technique to actors at a large classical repertory theatre, the Stratford Festival Theater, in Stratford, Canada. I am employed by the theatre as a integral part of a support staff or coaching team, made available as a resource for the actors. The actors come to the classes because they are looking for tools and techniques to solve specific theatrical movement or vocal problems.

In the theatre world, the Alexander teacher is there to serve the actor. The actor serves the play. The requirements and challenges of the play and the rehearsal process are ever present when working with an Alexander teacher. Every day, I teach actors during the creative process of rehearsal, seeing them through to the production and run of the show. We rehearse in a repertory programme, which means an actor can be involved in three different plays at any one time.

The theatrical experience is live and transitory. The risks an actor takes every night in the theatre are what make the experience exciting for an audience. Since the physical body is the actor's instrument of expression, it is vital that he is tuned in and aware of his corporeal versatility and flexibility. The Alexander work will heighten the actor's awareness of his physical habits and stimulate the actor's consciousness of how he may redirect his energy.

The Alexander Technique teacher can help the actor with both self-discovery and character discovery. A character has to evolve out of the actor's mind, body and emotions, reside there truthfully and experience the story of the play or film, moment by moment. The greater the actor's sensitivity and awareness of his body, the wider the range of choices or responses he can make for himself and his characters. A lack of awareness of physical habits of tension can impede anyone, from the surgeon to the day-care worker. For the actor, the body is a creative instrument, which requires fine-tuning, finesse and precision.

There are many obvious physical challenges in staging a play, ranging from stage combat, period dancing and costuming to the physicality of farce. The subtle emotional life of the character on stage is also realized physically, through the body and voice of the actor. The actor's body needs stamina, agility, vocal power, emotional energy, vitality and authenticity to meet the demands of theatre.

My work over the years has been a fascinating investigation of the physical needs and problems of the actor. Actors have given me a great deal of insight into how and why the principles of the Alexander Technique are helpful in the acting process. It has been a collaborative exploration of Alexander's work and, together, we have discovered how the Alexander Technique helps the actor's physical coordination achieve difficult staging or characterization. For this reason, the reader will also hear how the Alexander work applies to specific questions of movement and voice from the actor's perspective.

It is my hope that this book will give the reader an inside look into the Alexander Technique as it is relevant to the creative acting process in theatre and film. I trust that the aspiring young actor will learn from the experienced, seasoned veteran about the daily diet and discipline of a life in the theatre. I relish working with all stages of an actor's training, and, in my experience, teaching movement to a professional is not unlike working with a student. Students should be trained and treated like professional actors, just as professionals need to continue to study and learn throughout their careers. Mastering the acting craft is an ongoing endeavour; therefore, a serious actor must be a student for life.

I also wish to encourage experimentation with some of the warm-up exercises and movement work laid out in the following chapters. These exercises are rooted in the Alexander work, but they are not the Alexander Technique. Let me qualify this by pointing out that the suggested physical exercises are for a healthy, active person who wants to experiment with a step-by-step process that is commonly practised in the warm-up of both the working and the student actor. The partnered movement work is more physically challenging and is recommended for an actively training actor or a drama-school teacher.

It is in the spirit of self-discovery and stepping into the unknown that I hope the reader will process this information. There is a good deal of actor movement work and exercises that I have developed over my years of teaching in the theatre. This text is not a purist study of the Alexander Technique. My emphasis has always been in the application of the Alexander principles to the performance problems of the actor. The focus of this book is on the acting craft and how the Alexander Technique can support the actor's exploration and use of the body in the work.

Let me note that throughout the book I have used the terms 'actor' and 'actress' when specifically quoting an individual artist. However, in general usage I have used the term 'actor' and the word 'he' – as opposed to 'actor/actress' and 'he/she' – as I felt this was the most efficient form for discussing an actor's process.

You simply cannot learn the Alexander Technique from a book. You can read about the concepts and principles of Alexander work, but at some point it is absolutely necessary to engage with a trained and certified Alexander Technique teacher. There are many Alexander teachers all over the world. To learn the Alexander Technique, one has to gain the knowledge of the unfamiliar and unhabitual through a guided experience. Alexander Technique teachers are knowledgeable and have highly skilled hands with which to introduce the student to a new kinesthetic experience of the body. When one takes the initiative to learn something unknown, it is inestimably helpful to have a guide who can indicate options and encourage discovery. The exploration of the 'unknown' is a necessary risk in the learning process. There is not a right way to learn the Alexander Technique, nor can you master the Alexander Technique on your own without a teacher, but this book serves as an introduction to why and how we are using the Technique in the theatre world today.

F. M. Alexander's Story

F. M. Alexander (1869–1955) was an actor, and he was passionate about the art form of theatre. Frederick Mathias Alexander was born in Wynyard, Tasmania, Australia. He became an impassioned actor of classical dramatic literature, particularly reciting Shakespeare. He took lessons in drama and elocution with the most reputable teachers that Melbourne had to offer. Within a few years, Alexander had established himself in the Melbourne theatre scene through his productions of plays and dramatic recitals, but found he was losing his voice during performance. Alexander consulted a variety of doctors who recommended remedies and treatments. Unable to diagnose his problem, they all suggested rest. But afterwards, as soon as he went back to performing, he consistently experienced hoarseness and chronic vocal fatigue.

Alexander had studied voice training and knew about breathing techniques such as diaphragmatic and intercostal breathing and the then current fashion of vocalizing styles, but he realized that none of the exercises or techniques helped him to preserve and protect his voice production.

Ever the keen and observant actor, Alexander began to experiment, noting exactly what he did with himself when he was reciting verse. He set up three mirrors to enable him to observe himself 'in the round' and proceeded to speak. He noticed a pattern. Every time he began to recite, he pulled his head backwards, depressed the larynx, took breath through his mouth and audibly gasped for air. He discerned that this contraction of his head, back and downwards, would compress his larynx and create the gasping in his breathing. He also saw a tightening of his neck and shoulder muscles and tension in his jaw and facial mask. He realized that, in fact, he was doing something that was interfering with the vocal mechanism, thereby causing tension and strain on his voice. Eureka! But how was he to correct this habitual pattern in his speaking? He became aware of the relentless persistence of his habit of contracting his head and neck muscles despite his desire not to do so. He focused his attention on the moment he started speaking and he paused just before the habitual pattern could re-occur. In that sustained moment, he was able to make the choice not to proceed with his habitual pattern. It was in that moment of free-dom from the habitual response that Alexander applied his thinking to direct his neck to be free and to release his head to move forward and upwardly. This procedure of staying attentive to his body – of not succumbing to the habit of tightening the neck, while maintaining a mental commitment to the freedom and flexibility in his head, neck and spine throughout the activity of speaking – helped him regain the use and control of his voice. Thus he developed his own methodology or technique for freeing his voice and this was the beginning of the Alexander Technique.

Alexander moved to Sydney, opened an Academy for Voice Studies and began to teach voice production and breathing to singers and actors. His teaching experience evolved along with his exposure to a wide spectrum of students. The medical community gained awareness of the benefits of Alexander's work and doctors began to refer patients to him with problems ranging from tuberculosis to spinal ailments. Alexander's reputation grew, and he was soon inundated with stu-dents with a variety of problems.

Alexander started to understand the broader importance of his dis-covery. He was learning to re-educate the whole self in every activity. Like many inventors with a new and exciting idea, Alexander gave his initial experiment a trial run within his immediate family. Alexander had a brother, Albert Redden, who, like F. M., was known by his ini-tials, as A. R. Alexander. F. M. Alexander shared his innovative ideas with his brother, and A. R. joined F. M. in the development of a teach-ing method which involved using their hands to excite a new kines-thetic experience in the body of the student.

He set sail for London, England, in 1904 with his insight and hopes to teach the world his new method, the 'Alexander Technique'. Alexander quickly made his mark in London. The turn of the twentieth century was a wonderfully rich and creative period. F. M. Alexander was a participant in the global consciousness that was artistically and intellectually innovating and challenging the world's views. The theatre was rich and lively, this was the time of Chekhov, Stanislavsky and the Moscow Art Theatre, Ibsen, Artaud and Cocteau. The psycho-spiritual field was developing, introducing the ideas of Freud, Jung and Gurdjieff and the novels of Aldous Huxley. A vigorous visual art world brought Futurism, Expressionism and the emergence of cinema. The concept of 'consciousness' was in vogue. The world was ready for the Alexander Technique, which offered a unique method to address consciousness through the physical body that was both practical and effective.

Alexander set up residence and taught at 16 Ashley Place, London SW1, near Victoria Station. The theatre world embraced Alexander's work and soon many famous actors and performers were taking lessons. Among his roster of students were Sir Henry Irving, Beerbohm Tree and his theatrical family and George Bernard Shaw. Alexander was frequently seen in the wings of theatres in the West End, checking that his students were applying his method on stage and not falling into their old habits of contracting their heads and compressing the neck.

Shaw and Aldous Huxley wrote about the importance of the Alexander Technique and were terrific promoters of F. M. Alexander's work. In fact, George Bernard Shaw left money in his will to the RADA to initiate the Alexander Technique into the curriculum. F. M. Alexander the actor would be thrilled to see his work being carried on in the theatre. A man of the theatre before actor-training schools even existed, he would be proud to see Alexander forming a fundamental part of the curriculum in modern drama schools. The Alexander Technique is taught at the Guildhall School of Music and Drama, the Royal Academy for Dramatic Arts and LAMDA in London; the Juilliard in New York City; the American Conservatory Theater School in San Francisco; UCLA in Los Angeles; and the National Theatre School in Montreal, Canada; as well as in many other drama schools.

PART I
The Alexander Technique in the Theatre

How the Alexander Technique Became My Vocation

My understanding and study of movement is based on the Alexander Technique. From the age of six, I was involved in amateur theatre. My most fulfilling hours in high school were rehearsing and performing school plays. Then, like many teenagers, lost in liberal arts, I found myself enrolled in a general theatre studies programme at the University of Toronto. There, I was introduced to the modern theories of the stage, including those of Stanislavsky, Grotowski, Meyerhold, Artaud and Brecht.

I went off to San Francisco in the late 1970s to witness the post-hippie movement of Haight-Ashbury, the pre-Aids heyday of gay liberation and to experience a 6.0 earthquake! My naive Canadian consciousness was raised beyond my expectations.

I was only twenty-two years old when I undertook the three-year Alexander teacher-training course under the guidance and direction of Frank Ottiwell. He is an actor as well as an Alexander teacher. Frank's Alexander Technique teacher-training school is located at the American Conservatory Theater in San Francisco. Frank was a member of the ACT acting company and also taught in the conservatory actor-training programme. Frank was a brilliant mentor for me. He taught me a way of applying the Alexander work directly to the acting training process. At that time, there was no other Alexander Technique teacher-training course in the world that offered both a master teacher in the Alexander Technique and Ottiwell's theatrical experience. In the last half of my training Frank brought me along to observe, and then to assist, him teaching his Alexander classes with the acting programme. Frank prepared me to focus and marry my love of the theatre with my Alexander teaching.

Frank Ottiwell invited other master teachers to come to his school and share their expertise. Patrick Macdonald came from England annually while I was training. He had been trained by F.M. Alexander in the 1930s and his teaching style was very disciplined and seemed quite formal to me. He was one of the early teachers who felt that Alexander had passed down the mantle of his work to him. About fifteen years ago a series of international congresses was instituted that have been held from Australia to Israel, and points between, bringing together Alexander teachers who might otherwise never have met or worked together. They have been instrumental in opening communication and have gone a long way towards saving the Alexander world wasting its energy in petty protectionism and other politics.

It was in early 1978 that Frank Ottiwell and his training class made their first connection with Marjorie Barstow, then a seventy-eight-year-old from the American heartland of Lincoln, Nebraska. 'Marj' had been on Alexander's first training course in London. Her teaching style was quite different from Patrick Macdonald's, though the basics were of course the same. What interested me about Marj's teaching was the fact that she taught in large groups while giving every individual a period of her full attention.

She placed an emphasis on applying the Alexander principles to performance and simple activities, and on encouraging all of the group participants to learn by improving their observation skills as they watched each other work. Marj challenged her students to be present and alert and to 'do some constructive thinking' to replace the more familiar kind of doing, which is usually pushy and abrupt, without breath or consideration. Marj taught this thinking process to the singer, the violinist, the flautist, the tennis player through to the aikido practitioner by applying the Alexander Technique directly to the activity. The knowledge and experience in her hands was profound and the changes that the student would undergo were fascinating to observe and to experience.

Marj's emphasis on 'delicacy' and the subtlety in her teaching made a big impact on Frank Ottiwell's work and, in turn, the training of teachers. At this point, my insight into the Alexander work was just beginning to take shape. Marj Barstow's teaching had a clear emphasis on movement. Her manner of observing and applying Alexander's principles directly to performing an activity was right up my theatrical alley. I studied extensively with Marj. The next few years of training were exciting and full of debate, as to what the Alexander Technique was and how it should be taught.

On April Fool's Day, 1980, I returned home to Toronto as a newly certified teacher of the Alexander Technique. At that time, only a few people were teaching this esoteric movement principle to the Canadian public. There was a virgin market in Canada for Alexander Technique teachers. There I was, just fresh out of school, green and keen. Fortunately for me, the Alexander Technique had already established a considerable worldwide reputation in the fields of music and theatre. Within a year, I was teaching at the Stratford Festival of Canada, the most prestigious classical repertory theatre in North America. I was dropped into a professional theatrical arena that embraced the notion of ongoing training for the actor. Now, nineteen years later, I realize I grew up teaching at the Stratford Festival. My teaching education developed in a 'hands-on' manner in response to the needs of the classical repertory actor. Finding my way to support and contribute to the theatrical process with the Alexander Technique has been a rewarding experience. Plugging into the professional theatre world at such an early stage in my career was a godsend, and it helped to shape and focus my teaching for actors in film and on stage.

The Alexander Teacher's Role in the Production of a Play

On the first day of rehearsal, an energized, outwardly positive group of artists, open and ready to leap into the adventure of storytelling, meets in the rehearsal hall. The enthusiasm is palpable, but one can't help but sense the undercurrent of terror. This group includes the entire cast of actors, maybe numbering more than thirty, the director, designer, composer, lighting designer, stage managers, fight director, choreographer, voice coach, movement and Alexander coach, as well as a production team of design and technical staff. The play will have a design and a conceptual plan which the director and designer will present to the group. There will obvious problems to solve. What is the period of the piece? Does the director see the play in a certain acting style? What will the costumes entail: corsets, robes, swords, veils, trains, wigs? Are there dialects? Is there a period dance or a sword fight? What about the venue: is the play staged on a proscenium, does it have a raked stage, or is it played in the round? How large an audience will fill the venue? All these questions will have answers to be worked out by a variety of experts and artists that make up the team of the theatrical collaboration.

Actors that I work with in Stratford come to the Alexander work from a wide range of training backgrounds. Although many of them have had previous experience with other Alexander teachers, it is unusual for them to have a teacher constantly available throughout the rehearsal process, when they are focusing on specific roles.

Each actor brings to the rehearsal a unique acting process and methodology. I have never found two actors who work in exactly the same way, so my challenge is to learn from them how they work. The classes are voluntary, the actors come because they choose to and they come with a variety of motivations. Each one has an individual physical history, deriving from the wear and tear that comes with a career in the theatre. Actors are keen to explore the Alexander Technique because an old injury haunts them, or they suffer issues of tension, or experience vocal fatigue, have a fear of falling when on stage, want to open up the chest, relax the jaw, take care of their knees, cope with ageing, arthritis or lower backache, or they simply want to tune in to their body.

For my part, as an Alexander teacher working for the theatre, it is my job to help solve the individual's movement problems as well as explore the physical problems that come with playing the character. On that first day of rehearsal, my attention will turn to the individual actors and the problems of playing their characters. I will consider the individual's personal movement and the vocal habits that they bring with them on the first day. I will observe the actor animal in his prosaic everyday mode, noticing how he uses his voice and body out of performance. I begin to gather information and observations prior to the actor's first class.

When the actor is scheduled for his first class, I will begin with a 'hands-on' introduction to the Alexander principle or a renewed acquaintance with the work in private, one-on-one tutorials with the actor. We will talk over their physical history -- i.e., whether they have any past injuries and what mode of fitness or exercise they practise -- and examine their awareness of problems of tension and physical or vocal habits. We will probably discuss how the actor is considering the physical life of the character and whether the play presents any movement problems, such as fainting, limping, running, fighting, costuming. We would proceed by applying the Alexander Technique to simple movements of walking, reaching, bending and speaking. This is a time to plant the seeds for change and to heighten awareness relative to the need of the actor. We embark on the work with goodwill and curiosity.

When rehearsals have been under way for several weeks, the actor will have established working relationships, good, bad or indifferent, with the director and fellow actors. The actor's character is beginning to take shape and he will be receiving some specific direction from the director in rehearsal. In private tutorial, the actor will receive technical and practical guidance from the Alexander teacher in order to achieve the actor's objectives for the character. At this point, the director may turn to the coaching staff for assistance and discussion of what the director would like to see from the actor in the play. The director may see some potential that the actor is failing to realize and will express his vision of the character. The coaching staff have the luxury of time outside the rehearsal room to focus privately with an actor on the perceived problem. This can provide the actor with more time to explore the dilemma away from the pressure of the rehearsal hall and hopefully to work out the problem under the objective eye and support of the teacher's expertise. For the actor, this might be the most exciting yet doubt-filled and frustrating period in the creative process: knowing what is wanted, staying open to direction and playing with options, and finding one's way through the play.

With the first dress rehearsal, all the elements of the theatricality of the production are brought together: the wigs, costumes, music, sound cues and lighting. Any big technical problems with the show will reveal themselves at this point. This is often a stressful and emotionally charged time, as it is the point when the director might make big changes. The director might cut a scene, song or dance, shorten a fight sequence, kill a costume, change sound or technical effects. It can be upsetting for actors to let go of a sequence or scene into which they may have invested their hearts, but it is exciting to see the many elements come together in the theatrical experience.

Mostly, the problems are of a technical nature. Often, the added element of costuming helps the actor bring the character to life. Details in movement and breath can often be affected by costuming such as corsets, shoes and hats. The actor will make adjustments and adapt. Often, after the first dress rehearsal, actors will come to me to work out the physical and technical issue of costuming. I might help them release some tension and find their breath in a problematic corset, adapt their balance to walk in a period shoe, or move more confidently and comfortably in a cape with a sword. There are many situations that upset an actor's balance. A raked stage can cause lower-back fatigue, and lifting or carrying another actor is always problematic.

Notes and reports about vocal clarity or audibility will begin. The specific technical details of movement or vocal problems will be processed with a voice or movement teacher. In Part 4, I will discuss how Alexander work can help to address a variety of technical issues for the actor.

By now, most decisions have been made by the actors and director, and the cast will feel the need for feedback from a live audience. At this point in rehearsal, most of the inside observers -- director, designer, coach or technical crew -- are overly exposed to the actors and the material. Especially in a comedy, the actors need exposure to fresh viewers, who will respond to the comedic business. They will be starved for an audience.

Now is the time to support the work that has been accomplished by the actor and to help build the confidence necessary to allow the actor to fly. In my experience, the actor needs to be nurtured and reinforced with positive energy. Judgement is trying, and most actors need a boost of self-confidence and reassurance. The Alexander teacher working in the theatre has to be flexible to accommodate actors' needs and process. It is important to allow the actor to ask for help and to set the learning agenda to his needs. The actor may continue to invite challenging input or may require a rest from processing feedback. The actor will want to feel a solid marriage with his character and ownership of the character's story.

As the actor meets the first audience in previews, he may be suffering from too much or too little input from the director. The actors will be processing too many opinions at this stage: the artistic director, producers, designers, dressers, voice coaches, movement coaches, other actors and publicity people will liberally share opinions of how they feel the play is going. This theatrical creative process can be fraught with anxiety and the need for approval. The old adage 'An opinion is like an asshole, everybody has one' is apropos when it comes to the difficulties of producing plays in repertory.

During the previews, the Alexander teacher can contribute a 'hands-on' input to calm the actor 's nerves and fraught energy. The seasoned actor will be using this initial contact with an audience to work on the finesse of the craft, focusing on the fine-tuning of a performance.

This is too often the period where injuries occur from over-fatigue or the actor pushing himself. The Alexander teacher will often be dealing with the ongoing problems of fatigue or stress in the actor's body from the physical demands of repertory theatre. The teacher can provide the actor with a maintenance programme for the body's well-being. Sometimes there is the unforeseen injury that can occur inside or outside the theatre. An actor may strain a muscle or fall off his bike en route to the theatre, and the Alexander teacher can be a helpful hand on the road to an actor's recovery.

Opening-night jitters are palpable. It is my job to offer a calming, quiet, lying-down table session to help the actor relax and connect with his breath and focus attention in the body. Staying composed in the body, allowing a connection to breathing is the best thing the actor can do for himself prior to an opening night.

I might add that the coaching staff also suffers from opening-night anxiety. When I watch the show, it is likely that I have had contact or input with most all the players on the stage. I must confess, I have sat in an opening-night audience holding my breath, tensing my neck, bursting with trepidation and goodwill for the players. It is a delicious sensation to sigh with relief during the curtain call and to burst forth with applause for your colleagues, knowing all the work that went into producing the evening.

My unique position as an Alexander teacher in the professional theatre has been endlessly interesting and ever-changing throughout the course of an extended repertory season. To do a good job of supporting the actor, the Alexander teacher should possess qualities of goodwill, sensitivity, objectivity, humour, prudence and generosity.

The Principles of the Alexander Technique

There are several concepts that one has to understand in order to be able to proceed and explore the Alexander Technique on one's own. It is no accident that the word 'technique' is used, as Alexander devised a methodology or procedure to follow in order to direct the body in a new direction and in a non-habitual manner. As we study the principles and concepts of learning the Alexander Technique, we shall see the direct relationship and application to the craft of acting. After all, Alexander made his discovery when searching for a solution to his theatrical vocal problems.

My teaching experience has been predominantly with the acting profession and therefore the focus in my teaching has been to discover how the Alexander Technique serves the actor and the process of acting.

This chapter deals with theory and, as with anything theoretical, it can only be properly understood through the practical application of the theory. It will be helpful to start by breaking down and explaining the principles of the Alexander Technique in order to understand the sequence or order of the concepts that make up the Alexander work.

1. Recognition of habit present in an activity or movement.
2. Inhibition. The idea of stopping or pausing to undo the unwanted habitual response to an activity.
3. The 'primary control'. The 'primary control' is observable in all animal movement. When a dog, horse, cat or lizard moves its head, it moves from the top of the spine in a forward and upward direction, which engages the spine to lengthen.
4. Giving direction. The notion of using your thinking to redirect your movement in an orderly sequence to mobilize the primary control.

5. Recognition of faulty sensory feedback. Learning that our kinesthetic sense is tied in to the habit, thereby giving unreliable sensory feedback in the early stage of the learning experience. Our feelings are accustomed to our habits. When we make a change, the nervous system responds with new sensations and we become unsure of our feelings.

6. End-gaining. The concept of the student being too focused on the end of a desired goal and not being 'in the moment'. In Alexander work, the actor's attention will be in the moment of the means whereby they achieve their end.

7. Non-doing. Moving with ease. The truthfulness of the adage 'less is more'. Observing the quality of movement.

1. Recognition of Habit

The first step in the process of change is the recognition of what it is you are doing. Is there a need to change? If so, can the actor identify whether the action is habitual? When does the force of habit determine the action? Does the actor struggle or interfere with the freedom and flow of the activity? How is the actor initiating the activity? All these questions require self-scrutiny. Taking a moment to heighten awareness of the body in action gives the actor a good deal of information. Consider these common habits that actors have observed and see if you can identify them in and relate them to your own body.

- When standing at ease, are you slouching, by contracting the head into the neck or collapsing in the chest and shoulders?
- Are you sitting in the hips? Is your upper body compressing the lower body on to the hips joints, causing the belly to push forward and the lower back to narrow?
- Are you standing predominantly on one leg and resting your upper body weight on one hip joint?
- Are your knees locked?
- Since taking note of yourself, are you now busy trying to self-improve?

● Are you pulling up by lifting your chest and pushing the shoulders back as a means of standing up straight?
● Does sucking in and holding the belly make you feel you are pulling your act together?
● Are you tightening the fingers?
● Do you like crossing your feet at the ankle?
● Is your habit touching your face and covering your mouth?
● Are you tightening your jaw and holding your breath?
● Do you have the habit of breathing through the mouth?

As every individual is original, these questions are endlessly interesting. Does all this attention make you feel uncomfortable in your body? Beginning to observe your habits can drive you nuts. Please stay open and playful with the information you are gathering about yourself.

Taking this process a step further, into movement, we can begin to observe our habitual response to initiating the movement of walking.

● When you begin to walk, what is your habit? Do you tend to lead from the hip joint?
● What direction does your head move when you begin to take a step? Does your head contract? Do you lead from the chin?
● Are your feet leading ahead of your torso? Is your upper body leaning backwards?
● Do you push down through your legs and into your feet to step off?
● Is there a notable tendency to contract your head and press downwards in your body when you move?

One will observe a wide range of subtle and tedious habits. Even with the desire to change and a heightened awareness of a habit, the actor may learn from the director, the Alexander teacher or perhaps a fellow actor that he is repeatedly performing an action or a vocal pattern in a habitual manner. The actor will discover the need to confront the force of habit. Habit is a formidable force to oppose. Having identified a habit that causes tension or downward pressure in your body, what do you do now?

2. Inhibition – Pausing for an Instant to Arrest a Habit

Have you ever quit smoking or stopped biting your nails? If so, then you know that one must actively decide to stop and confront the habit in order to change a behavioural pattern. It takes discipline and consciousness to derail a habit.

In the Alexander Technique, the teacher will use the term 'inhibition'. The Alexander notion of inhibition signifies the idea of stopping a particular behaviour, to retard or prevent a habitual activity. We must not confuse the word 'inhibition' with a Freudian interpretation of the word, which proposes a suppression of emotion or desire suggesting a behavioural fear or lack of self-confidence to perform an action.

In the Alexander work, the concept of 'inhibition' is one of actively and consciously being aware of our response to a stimulus: for example, standing up, sitting down, speaking, reaching for the phone and then pausing or stopping. The actor will discover that if he pauses and opens the moment for a fleeting instant of awareness, other options will arise and he will undo a habit. The actor applying inhibition allows a moment of stillness, where the unknown will be experienced, which invites something else to happen other than the habit.

We all struggle with habits. The actor may have a habit of sitting in his hips, or gasping breath through the mouth, pushing his chin out when making an argument, or locking his knees. Whatever the habit, once the actor takes responsibility for recognizing his habit and then consciously says 'no' or consents not to repeat it, he proceeds into the unknown. It is there, in the moment of actively choosing the unknown and not responding with our habitual preconceived notions, that we allow ourselves to discover the many options of 'yes'. It is a novel idea for the actor to observe a habitual response and consciously decide not to act on it. One must be willing to let go of familiar expectations.

For example, as I am writing here at my computer, I make a spelling error. My response is to tighten my neck, creating excess tension in my shoulders, arms, fingers and legs. If I practise what I preach, at the next error I will notice my response, which is to contract my neck muscles, and I will consciously think 'No, don't clamp your neck. Instead, free the neck, release the head to move forward and upward.' I may discover that I can perform the action of typing without the tension. My momentary awareness of the habit gives me the opportunity to make a choice either to proceed habitually or to engage my thinking to direct my body to make a change.

If habit is a routine or a repetitive choice, then the actor is limiting options. If the actor wants to break new ground, to open up the alternatives and apply a varied palate to acting, learning what habits or patterns are blocking and limiting the spectrum of choices will need to come first. By using Alexander's principle of 'inhibition', the actor may observe a tension and make the choice to release that tension or to move in another way, thereby breaking up a set of physical patterns.

Every actor ought to become aware of his idiosyncratic manner in order to change it and make it easier to adopt a character. The character will have its own quirks. Acting is all about making choices. The rehearsal process is an experiment with a multitude of choices, allowing the actor to try out an array of emotions and physical choices in order to transform into the character. All actors go about this operation in their own unique ways. The actor's process, from the first rehearsal through to the opening night, is as wildly varied as each actor is individual. Some actors are very physical in their approach to a character and they will make many choices through the body, as if wrestling with the text and the character, whereas another actor may have a quiet, more interior struggle as they explore the text and recreate the story. The rehearsal period represents the fascinating journey of the human spirit's struggle to tell the truth.

In this search for the 'other', the actor will talk about 'getting out of the way' in order to allow the character to emerge and embody the story. Inhibition can be a wonderful tool to help the actor to 'get out of the way'. There will be countless opportunities in rehearsal for the actor to utilize this technique of inhibition. Breaking a habitual pattern by pausing and allowing a subtle and momentary change in the body may alter the actor's perception of how the character is experiencing the action in a scene. When the actor restores his mind and focus to the body, often the emotional and imaginative life of the character can be freed up. Since the body is always present and is ultimately the home one inhabits for every emotional experience, when the actor calls attention to the body, the whole situation is seen afresh. The body is a marvellous ally for the actor because it bears witness and tells the truth.

One actress describes her version of using the concept of inhibition in her rehearsal process:

> In my acting, I will become aware of a little habit, clock it and the next time it reappears, I'll take a moment's awareness and then replace it with a new way of thinking or a new way of moving. I check the habit and let it go, or I think, you just did what you are used to doing, let it go. I guess that is a process of saying 'No, don't do that'. For me, the Alexander Technique is like the process in meditation or thinking and becoming aware of your thoughts. It is not that I say 'Don't do it , stop it , stop that thought, stop that action', it is that you are aware of what you are doing, not to judge yourself or slap your wrists, just that you are simply aware of what you are doing. If you want to redirect yourself, then you do. The thinking process in the Alexander Technique should be knitted with the actual moving process, which is forward, up and out. An improvisation will stop if you say 'No . . . but'. However, it moves forward if you say 'Yes . . . and'. 'Yes, I am sitting in my old way and I am going to change that now' is better than 'Oh, you are sitting in the wrong way. Stop that, change it.' If you present the improvisational idea 'The sky is falling' and it is met with 'No it is not', then the story dies. It will stay alive if you say 'The sky is falling . . . I have an umbrella'. In my way of thinking, actors have so many judgements placed upon us, day to day in rehearsal, from the director or the designer, and often you are highly critical of yourself. The more support you can give yourself, the better. I see utilizing the Alexander Technique is to enable one. It is not to restrict or constrict or limit your choices but to widen the field for the actor. I like to think of it as a positive process. If you are prone to ruminating on a thought, there is that elastic-band theory of, as soon as you start to think about it you snap the elastic band and it tells you 'I'm thinking that again, move on'. I prefer to think of inhibition as rechannelling or redirecting or constructive thinking.

In acting, the actor wants to be sensitive and to listen to impulses that arise within himself in a dramatic situation. An impulse is viewed as an authentic response in the body which can inform the actor. It is important for the actor to be sensitive to the life in his body as the story unfolds. It is through both the mental and physical energy of the actor that he senses the character and opens up to the experience of being the other. This journey of becoming another character happens within both the mind and the body. I do not divorce the mind and the body. They are so interconnected that they work as complements to each other.

The concept of inhibition is a key principle in understanding the Alexander Technique. In an Alexander lesson, the teacher will suggest saying 'No' or stopping the student's initial or habitual impulse, in order to rid the actor of patterns and to allow a redirection of energy in a new and unfettered manner. The concept of inhibition as a tool for the actor can be controversial, because most actors strive to open themselves up to sense their impulses as a means of connecting to the character. They can be alarmed and dubious of the notion of stopping an impulse or sensation in the body. The Alexander teacher wants to be careful that the negative semantics of introducing the idea of inhibition do not turn the actor off. No actor wants to be ruled by habit, but they do want to heighten their impulses and listen to the emotional responses as they experience them in their bodies.

It is through the body that the actor is able to access an emotional state time and time again in a scene. It is important for the actor to understand that inhibition can be practised as a tool to derail further habits, offering a moment to make choices. It should never become a negative mental game of saying 'No' that will only shut off instincts and mislead one into thinking that there is a single right choice.

The actor must decide what change is wanted in a situation, be it physical or emotional, and then notice the response to the stimulus in a given situation. The next step is actively to give consent not to respond habitually, but instead to pause for a moment, permitting an unknown possibility to present itself. In this way, the actor is saying 'Yes' to other available experiences. Whenever we discover something new, we have to step into the unknown. It is important for the actor to have a flexible and open-minded process.

When asked about the Alexander Technique's concept of inhibition, a young actress responded:

> I have had the experience where I have an impulse to do something and just before I do it, I am aware of it. I feel my habitual impulse to pull my head back and down and I'm able to say, 'OK, that's what I feel; however, it is not necessary to follow through on it.' Or I think, I have a choice, I can proceed with the impulse or I can wait and see what happens if I don't . It is interesting to see what happens when I don't do the thing that I usually do, if I can catch that moment where I have the impulse before I have done the action. That's my concept of Alexander's inhibition.

Once the student is familiar and practised with the Alexander Technique, then this redirection in the body can happen in a split second. The mental process offers the tools to enable him to make choices to use the body efficiently and freely. A versatile and nimble actor will take a new direction and step into the unknown and untried in order to extend boundaries. I have admired actors in the rehearsal process who will try a new direction. Perhaps the director has an idea that is diametrically opposed to the actor's previous choice and yet, by allowing an open mind and agile body, the actor can inhibit his original choice, turn on a dime, embrace the director's idea and create a new approach to the scene. When the actor uses inhibition as an acting tool, it allows more choices into the process and the actor remains open to the exploration of the character and the play, and to life itself.

3. The 'Primary Control'

The 'primary control' is a concept that natural scientists have observed in all animal movement. Consider how animals move: their heads move freely at the neck. Their heads initiate movement from the top of the spine, in a forward and upward direction. It is perceivable that in an animal's movement, the balance or poise of the head to the spine has a forward and upward relationship. If you consider a giraffe running, its small head will move forward and upward, away from the top of its very long neck; the domestic cat will lead with its head when it jumps up on to a table, or the racehorse will win a race 'by a nose' by extending its head from the top of its spine to cross the finish line.

When we watch a beautiful mover, the 'primary control' will be evident in his action. Becoming aware of the concept of the primary control in one's movement and learning to employ thought to enhance this natural process is key to understanding the Alexander Technique. I recall watching my daughter as a very small infant struggling to find control of her head. Momentarily she would find the forward and upward poise of her head, giving her a fleeting connection to her backbone as if she could sit up by herself. As she progressed developmentally, her 'primary control' gave her control of her torso, supported an access to her arms and hands and developed further, to her feet and legs. It seemed that in no time we were watching her raise herself up and -- boom! -- she was off and walking. Next time you see a toddler in the park who is learning to stand and walk, observe the poise of its head in relationship to the spine. It is remarkable to see how alert and beautifully balanced the rather large head of a child is on top of its small body. The child uses its whole back and bends notably from the hip joints. The graceful ease in the quality of early childhood movement is wonderful.

One film actor said:

An awareness of the primary control has helped me, because I have a tendency to jut my chin out and push my head too forward, which does hideous things to the back of my neck. This can cause constriction in my throat and lungs, making it difficult to breath properly. I don't want to conversely pull my head down because I know my audience won't be able to see my eyes. Bottom line is, the awareness is there for me to use, the Alexander Technique helps me to keep a close eye on my habit. It is important for the actor to have precision in movement. In film, you might have to repeat something ten times and your body needs to be exact. Maintaining a free head and neck helps the actor achieve precision with freedom.

4. Giving Direction – Learning to Use Your Thinking to Make a Change

Having considered animal movement, one has to ask who is king of the forest? Human beings can use their minds and engage their thinking to change their movement. Unlike most animals, we do not have to rely on our instincts to survive. Certainly we use our instinct, yet we go further and use our thinking to survive.

In Alexander work, we can direct our thinking to mobilize the 'primary control'. The consciousness of a habit is the first step, followed by inhibition, pausing a moment to undo the habit. Now the actor can proceed with a constructive thought process and choose to redirect his body. The actor must use his thinking to direct his neck to be free; to release his head in a forward and upward direction; to allow an upward direction in his body. This thought process or technique allows the actor to decompress and release the downward pressure in his body. The quality of movement will change and lighten as the actor releases the tension and compression in his activity. Alexander described the human being's ability to apply his thinking to redirect the body as 'conscious constructive control of the use of the self'.

Once the actor becomes attentive to his habitual pattern and learns to undo his habitual response to a stimulus and uses his constructive thinking to allow a change, it will improve skills. Any tool that provides an actor with more options and choices will enhance and enliven the acting. Actors love to take physical and emotional risks, but they need to feel that they are in control of the mind and body to ride the edge, night after night.

There is nothing absolute in the Alexander learning process; it is a life sentence of self-observation and applied experimentation. The beauty of the Alexander Technique is that you can take it along into learning any new skill or technique involving coordination. No matter what contorted shape or heightened emotional state the actor finds himself in, he will be helped by thinking of freeing his neck at the occipital joint to recruit the primary control. It is a mental order, a sequential thought, and the thought is: to allow the neck to be free, to allow the head to release forward and upward, to allow the back to lengthen and widen. This sequential mental process, once experienced and understood, can instantaneously effect an easier quality in movement.

The direction 'up' can be applied to any movement or position and shape we may find ourselves. If I am tugging away, pulling off my winter boots and reeling about on one leg, the direction of 'up' will help me to elevate off my hip joints and release my bending torso upwards, improving my balance and control. Thinking 'up' can help if, for example, you are bending over to get something out of your car, or when you are stretching and reaching for your purse. The notion of upwards can help one to open and extend with a sense of the voluminous design of the body and all its parts. Later in this chapter, we shall do some practical exercises to experiment with applying these principles of the Alexander Technique to an actor's warm-up.

An actor's training and the demands of the profession are constantly changing. An actor needs tools to think constructively as he faces the wide variety of physical challenges that arise in the repertoire of dramatic literature. A young, yet seasoned, actor, who had the benefit of Alexander work throughout his training, said:

The Alexander Technique is a thinking process. I think it is called a technique because it is something that you continue to develop. It is one thing to become technically proficient, but if you want to master whatever it is you are doing, you have to keep at it, and keep developing it, changing your technique as you change as well. The reason I have the awareness is because I continue to think about it. When the Alexander teacher points out something that is going on in my body, then I go through a mulling-over process: 'OK, where is that? What does that feel like? What do I observe when I apply the Alexander Technique? What is it I am doing that is preventing me from taking care of that?' Once you figure that out, you literally have to continue to practise. It is hard to remember the first few times, because it is not just knowing it intellectually, it's also kinesthetic, it's physically experiencing it. Connect the thought with the physicality and eventually you can recognize it yourself when you slip back into the habit or problem. It is very much body, mind and emotion. You're thinking, you're sensing physically, and it enables you to connect in acting.

Another actor lets us in on his thoughts of his acting process:

Alexander gives you a self-diagnostic way to go back to check and assess the body. I need more breath, but my toes are clenching and so the balance is off there. If I play full out, and I reach a place where I think I'm going to have a meltdown, where I think my brain is going to explode, when I can't get enough oxygen and I can't get enough space, I assess in the moment and simply go in my body and find the freedom. When, in the last moments of Cyrano, I need an extra resource, or in the last three minutes of the fight in Hamlet, where does one find the extra bit of energy? It's not just burning on empty, it is not an endless reserve of energy, it's a mental energy that has a physical life. I can assess the situation and whatever part of the body isn't cooperating will send back a damage report and I will fix it. And I will fix it instantly and that's what I like about the Alexander Technique.

One actress, Rita Howell, who has also trained as an Alexander teacher, talks about the idea of giving oneself direction.

My work as an actor was vastly improved by the use of the Alexander Technique, not only physically but mentally and emotionally. In terms of giving myself Alexander's direction, I do think that it's my job to know where my head is in relation to my body. To recognize those times when I revert to habit, which I don't think you are ever fully free of, it is always constantly remembering to remember. The greatest value that I found with the Alexander work for myself as an actor was that it changed my emotional and mental approach to my work. I found that my thinking about my work became clearer as my thinking about my body became clearer. My process for preparing for a role is more efficient, is more enjoyable and I am much better prepared when I go into the rehearsal. As I lost some of the habits in the use of my body, I lost the habits of my relationship to my work with the constraining neurotic habits. Then when I free myself from tension and anxiety, I am able to connect with the subtext more easily so that when I start the rehearsal process I have a whole bunch of stuff there. I have not locked myself into a concept which does not allow something to happen or something to change in the work. Actually during performance and in the rehearsal process, I'm much clearer in my thinking, which doesn't mean to say I don't tie myself up again and again, but I can now recognize it and say 'Oops, what am I doing?' and then make a little change, a small change. I would observe where the hell my head was in relation to my body and I would think about my whole body and think about getting my whole body into moving upward. Allowing a bit of ease to take place is just a small change, but then I find myself thinking better.

5. 'Feelings' May Give Unreliable Feedback

If and when we apply the Alexander principle, we must be open to feelings of unfamiliarity in order to explore a change. Our feelings are tied into many years of a habit. We become accustomed to the sensations we experience when we move in our habitual way. When we make a change and move differently, our kinesthetic sense is habituated to our customary sensations. Our perception of the change may be faulty or unreliable, as our only point of reference is the sensation of our habit.

When you work with an Alexander teacher, their hands will give you a stimulus to move in a new direction. When the student initiates a movement by thinking of freeing the neck and allowing his head to move forward and upward along with the guidance of the teacher's hands, there will be a change in the movement pattern and the student will probably have an agreeable sensation of lightness and length in the body. One's first Alexander class is usually a pleasant experience of ease and lightness in the body.

Of course, one wants to be able to recreate that experience on one's own. When you begin to work on yourself and start thinking about Alexander direction without the teacher's involvement and energy, then the kinesthetic feedback will be different.

If you observe what you are doing, and pay attention to the quality and direction of your movement, there will be a sensory element and feedback that is informative. However, I always caution the student, when they begin to apply the work by themselves, not to compare or seek the same kinesthetic experience they have had with the teacher. The reason for this is that in the Alexander lesson with the teacher, there are two energies involved in the dynamic of the movement which effects the kinesthetic feedback. Therefore, to avoid confusion, simply focus on your thinking when applying the Alexander Technique and not on your feelings. As you apply the Alexander thinking, your sensitivity to the quality of movement will constantly be changing.

I asked a new class of young actors, 'What did you notice about your movement after your introductory Alexander Technique class?' One actress responded:

> I was surprised when I paid attention to the way I walked that I did find I was leading from my hips and leaning back. And I said to my husband, 'The movement teacher said I lead from the hips' and he said, 'Yeah, I know, you always do.' I didn't have a clue that I moved like that. I looked in the mirror and when I came forward and upward I felt dramatically forward and I felt like the Hunchback of Notre Dame, but to my surprise, I could see in the mirror that I didn't look like that.

6. End-gaining

One of our great habits when approaching the learning process is attempting to 'get it right' immediately. We fail to value the struggle of learning and experimentation with the unknown. How can we be right when we do not know what we are doing? We fear getting it wrong. We want to attain an end and have something to show for our effort. Alexander used the term 'end-gaining' to express this idea of being overly conscious of achieving the end of an action. This tendency to focus on the end interferes with the 'means whereby' the action is performed. Often, in an Alexander lesson, the student will be asked to observe himself moving in and out of a chair. When confronted with the stimulus to stand up, the student will most likely have a habitual response to that stimulus. Perhaps the student's response is to point the chin up and contract the head back and downwards on the neck. This is an example of end-gaining, standing up by indicating where you want to go, by initiating the action of standing by leading from the chin. The 'means whereby' is the 'how' we achieve the action. When the student is able to think of freeing the neck, releasing the head to lead forward and upward, and allowing the whole body to follow the head, then he will move with ease up on to the legs. To make a change, the student inhibits the impulse to end-gain and instead engages some constructive thinking by staying conscious of the means whereby the action of standing up is achieved.

For example, if I dive into a swimming pool to swim a mile and then, halfway down the pool, begin to count lengths before I have even touched the end of the pool, this reveals that I am not in the moment of the swimming. Instead, I am way ahead of where I am realistically. Staying with the 'means whereby' would focus my attention on the extension of my arms, the freedom in my neck as I move my head to take a breath, the flexion and rotation in my hip joints and the lengthening of my leg as I flutter-kick. *Voilà!* I arrive at the end of the pool having achieved one step in the means whereby I swim a mile. Paying attention to the quality of my movement when performing an action will help my understanding of what is involved in the movement as well as how I might find ease and efficiency in performing the action.

This principle of 'end-gaining' is very relevant to the acting process, as the actor strives to be truthful and alive in the moment. The actor must remain open and stay fresh in the storytelling. Let us take, for example, the scene in *Hamlet* when Laertes returns home to Elsinore to challenge the prince, having learned the news of his father's death, and is then confronted with his sister Ophelia's madness. The range of his emotional journey runs the gamut of rage, shock, sadness, grief and vengeance. All of these emotions have physical parallels; they are experienced in the body as much as in the mind. The actor will need to examine and endure every emotional change and realization through the body. The actor playing Laertes will need to observe many physical responses: rhythmic modulation of his breathing, all the muscular tension and urges to release energy. This costs the actor: he is challenged to stay open to the moment as the scene unfolds or his performance will become an emotional muddle. Being alert in his body will help him journey through the progression and building of the scene. In recreating this story night after night, the actor will have to apply 'inhibition' to help him to stay in the moment and not to 'end-gain' and play the emotions that unfold at the end of the scene.

One actor describes the process:

> In a dramatic situation, you stand a better chance of getting some-where valuable or valid if you do not try and decide intellectually what the end should be. You limit your exploration if you have decided where it will end. For then you have prescribed a journey that will be consequently dull for you and for everybody else. You must have faith to believe that the end, whatever it may be, if approached by this road of 'not end-gaining', will have a clearer site than by any other [route]. How do we create the experience and be truthful after acting in four productions of *Romeo and Juliet* and still say 'I don't know how it is going to end'? How do I believe, as Romeo, that I am never going to die and everything will work out fine? One time, in rehearsal with fight director B. H. Barrie, I was playing Romeo in the crypt with Paris, the fight comes up and we fight, fight, fight, and Paris disarmed me. However, Paris doesn't arrest Romeo, what is going on? We were playing a different ending and Paris was leading me out of the crypt through the gate and then I got out of the gate a millisecond before Paris, and I turned around and whacked him in the head with the gate and -- boom! -- we were off to somewhere else and the story continued. It is just that moment of: what? Where are we? We have never experienced this before, this is all new, that makes acting so exciting. The Alexander notion of 'end-gaining' is right on, if actors are asked to do that journey every night, why not take along a few tools so you have a more secure foundation from which to go find it.'

A young actress describes her struggle with the Alexander thinking and the concept of end-gaining:

> I like the Alexander idea of 'end-gaining' for acting, it's good to have a word that represents that the end result isn't all there is and that there is the 'means whereby' in the theatrical moment. Even though I see that I make mistakes, I'm starting to realize that

making mistakes is a big part of the learning. My habit is to try and get it right. In acting, if you are trying to be in the moment, you actually aren't in the moment because you are too busy trying to be in the moment. Truly discovering what is real in my acting comes without end-gaining. That is the way I like to be on stage, you just have to accept what the moment brings. When you are doing a play for a long run, it can be a fascinating laboratory, telling the same story again and again, because the experience of the now can be so rich or it can be so stale.

7. Non-doing – 'Less is More'

In the Alexander work, the student is encouraged not to try by physical exertion. The student is also asked not to rely on feelings to observe action, but instead to allow the student's thinking to redirect movement. Half the battle is refraining from pushing and straining and simply allowing the action to occur. One needs to analyse the quality of movement in the performance of an action. Is the quality of movement stiff, rushed, droopy, staccato, light or heavy? Once the quality of movement is assessed, then a choice can be made as to what is the appropriate or desired quality. Often we work too hard and tend to push and overdo an action. We joke in the theatre that this can lead to 'an overacting injury'. The concept of 'non-doing' is a means for allowing a new experience without the effort and stress of the habitual action. In acting and in the Alexander Technique, the old adage 'less is more' is desirable.

One actress observed:

What one strives to do in one's acting is less. Most actors have a tendency to start off pushing a bit too much and trying too hard. The Alexander notion of 'non-doing' is a great metaphor for acting, in that one can behave the way one wants to behave and do what you want to do, by actually not doing very much. Finding an efficient means of getting your point across rather than an over-exerted method is better for achieving an objective on stage.

When one leading actress with whom I had worked with for many seasons was asked if she applied the Alexander Technique in her acting, she replied:

> Oh yes, I always check in with my body before I go on stage. Having acted now for a number of years and having worked with both a voice teacher and an Alexander Technique teacher, I am conscious of all my bad habits. I know exactly where I put my tension, it has become all too familiar. I used to rely on energy to push past my awkward tensions. Now I know that the little twinge in the back of my shoulder cannot be blamed on the corset I'm wearing, it actually has to do with all the tension that I have focused right there in between my shoulders. I just need to release it before I go on stage. And indeed, once on stage, during a scene, when I notice that I am sticking my chin out to get my point across, it always gives me a sign that there is something wrong in the scene or in a particular moment because I'm having to push or force my argument. When I refrain from the pushing and release the tension, I look more attractive.

Reading about the concepts of the Alexander Technique, one may be daunted by the bulk of information. On paper, it may seem too cerebral a procedure simply to move with less tension and greater ease. However, I must reiterate that it is an educational process and it requires the input, guidance and objectivity of a trained Alexander Technique teacher. Once the student has been instructed and guided through the experience of the Alexander work, then they will be prepared to do the work for themselves. The aim of the Alexander teacher is to is to endow the student with a working awareness and problem-solving technique. The freedom of choice to apply the work is in the consciousness of the actor/student. A foundation in the Alexander Technique is a wonderful tool for the novice actor undertaking the challenging diversity of professional acting training.

The Anatomy Lesson

In order for the teacher to learn how the acting student perceives his own body, one must pose questions in basic anatomy. When I meet a group of actors for the first time, I ask the students the following questions:

- Where is the hip joint?
- What and where is the occipital joint?
- Where does the neck muscle attach to the skeleton?
- What muscles connect the arms to the body?
- Where are the lungs?

and so forth.

The conceptions the student has about the musculo-skeletal structure and how it functions are informative and are often reflected within the movement of the actor. It is interesting to ask students to draw the skeleton of their own bodies prior to examining any anatomy charts. The drawings, no matter how rudimentary, reveal the students' varied concepts and misconceptions of the body's proportion, structure and dimension. The notion of the structure of the body is often demonstrated in the actor's physicality or in the organization of the body structure. If the actor has a habit of sitting in the hips, he will tend to draw a shortness in the legs or an exaggeratedly large pelvis. No one will illustrate the accurate length of the spine and very few will position the spine in the centre of the skull.

Introduction to Anatomy with Diagrams

Let me take you through a simple, basic survey of the anatomy charts in order to share a reference to the body's bones and muscles. A mutual understanding of and reference to the anatomy will be helpful in movement exercises further on in the book. In my experience, when an actor thinks about the body in movement, he pays attention to the muscles, often forgetting the skeletal structure to which the muscles are attached. The muscles move the bones and the bones move the muscles; the marriage of the two is self-evident.

Let us begin by looking at the bones, referring to the diagrams of the three viewpoints of the skeletal system. From a design point of view, note what similarities can be observed about the upper and the lower limbs. The smaller the bones, the finer the dexterity, as we see in the use of the hands and the feet. We don't train or utilize the feet to the extent of the hands, but, if needed, the feet can be taught to perform many functions. Think of Daniel Day Lewis portraying Christie Brown in the film *My Left Foot*.

The wrists and the ankles are similar in design. By comparing both, one will observe a pile of jointed bones with two long bones extending up into one complicated joint, the elbow or the knee. From the elbow and the knee, a long singular bone progresses into a large ball-and-socket joint at both the shoulder and the pelvis. The butterfly-shaped pelvis is the biggest bone in the body. From the rear point of view, observe how the triangular-shaped bone, the sacrum, fits into the pelvis. The coccyx, or tail bone, is the bottom of the spine. If you have ever fallen on your tail bone, you will have experienced pain shooting straight up the spine. The space between the sit bones, the coccyx and the pubic bones, we shall call the pelvic floor. Note the changes in the shape of the vertebrae as your gaze travels up the spine.

When you look at the frontal view of the spine, you will observe the discs between the vertebrae. The function of the discs is to provide cushioning or shock absorption between the vertebrae. You will not see the discs from the rear-view perspective. The discs are located towards the front of the spine and the nervous system runs down the spine behind the discs. The forward location of the discs influences the body's balance and flexibility. When the torso is forward-balanced, over the legs, the body has more options to move and to absorb impact. The frontal location of the discs is the technical reason why a forward direction is desired in tennis, hockey, ballet barre, t'ai chi and most movement disciplines.

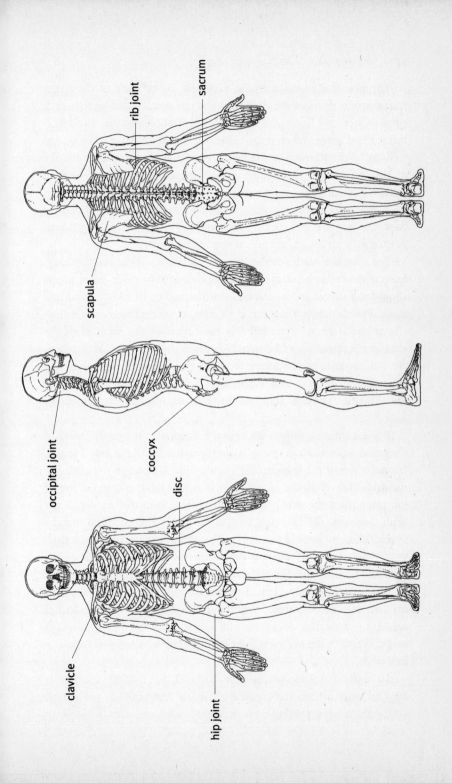

The ribs are jointed with the vertebrae at the back of the spine. Often people think of the ribcage as a single unit, forgetting that each rib is jointed and flexible. We can allow for more movement and flexion in the ribcage. When people think of sitting up straight, they tend to hoist up the sternum or the breast bone at the front of the ribs. Try it. You will observe a stiffening in the chest and that the movement in the ribs and backbone becomes restricted and breathing affected. I can hear my mother's voice saying 'Stand up straight, get your shoulders back and get that hair out of your eyes!' This command only motivated me to lift my chest and narrow my lower back.

The shoulder blades or the 'scapula' at the rear view and the 'clavicle' or the collar bone at the frontal view are the three joints of the shoulder, a simple snap-on arrangement attached by muscles and tendons. The clavicle is jointed at both ends. Placing a finger on the clavicle at the sternum, one will feel the action of the joint when the shoulder is raised up and down. Now trace the other end of the clavicle out towards the shoulder to sense the action of the joint. The movement of the ball-and-socket joint is more obvious. The joints of the shoulders provide ample movement potential and action in the arms.

While continuing up to the top of the spine, in the profile view of the skeleton, notice the spine's natural curvature. All the major joints, from the top of the spine to the ankles, line up through the centre of the body. Travel up the spine to the occipital joint, where the top of the spine joins the skull. The occipital joint is in the middle of the skull, between the ears and behind the eyes. The occipital joint is located directly behind the uvula. The uvula is that little bit of flesh that hangs down off the soft palate or the back of the roof of the mouth. Think of a cartoon character screaming and you will envisage the uvula as a punching bag at the back of the throat. This is a critical area for the Alexander Technique, because when the student is asked to 'free the neck, to allow the head to move forward and upwardly', the occipital joint is where the freedom and release is initiated.

All of the senses are processed in the head. Sight, smell, taste, hearing and voice are animal-survival attributes connected to perception and instinct. Most perception is processed in the region of the head. In a production of *Hamlet*, when the gravedigger gives Hamlet a skull – 'Alas, poor Yorick!' – the jaw bone should not be attached. The jaw is an appendage. The skull includes the top teeth, the cheekbones, around the earholes and the nasal cavity. The head weighs around ten to twelve pounds.

The respiratory system (the lungs), the vocal mechanism and the trachea are attached to the skeleton at the base of the skull. From there, the lungs, the larynx and the trachea are designed to suspend freely in the body. Downward compression of the head and neck can affect the proper functioning of these organs, causing interference in the remarkable suspension design.

If possible, observe the breathing of an infant and you will note a free and flexible apparatus, not to mention a fantastic big voice should the baby express its needs. With breath work, do not worry about making a connection to the rise and falling movement of the diaphragm because you cannot feel it. When you are breathing on support or breathing down, you have a sensation of the breath in the lower belly. What you feel moving with breathing is the engagement of the muscle of the abdominal wall. Breath is movement.

Take a look at the three viewpoints of the muscles on the following page. One can observe Alexander's notion of length and width in the design of the musculature. Muscles, tendons and cartilage are all considered connective tissue and work together intricately. Observe the latissimus dorsi, the biggest of the back muscles, and how it fans up from the buttocks and widens out to connect or insert into the bone of the upper inner arm. Note the origin or insertion of the neck muscle in the centre of the spine around the middle of the back. The muscle is V-shaped and fans up and outwards to support the head. There are many neck muscles which contribute to the support and wide range of movement in the head and neck. In the profile view, one sees the length and complex interconnection of the arm and leg muscles. In the frontal view is the abdominal wall and some indication of the inter-costal muscles that run diagonally around the ribs. The large pectoral muscles stretch across the chest from the sternum and insert into the upper arm. The arms are interconnected with the muscles of the front and back of the torso.

Cognizance of the interconnection of the muscles and the bones

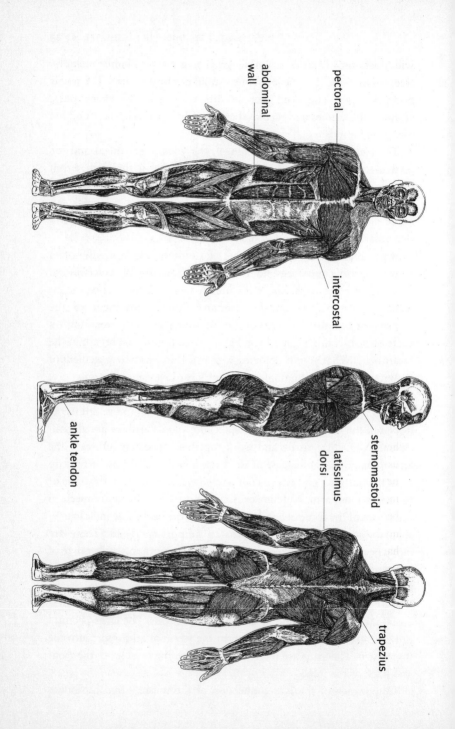

pectoral

abdominal
wall

intercostal

ankle tendon

sternomastoid

latissimus
dorsi

trapezius

will help you to comprehend the Alexander directions 'Let the neck be free, to allow the head to move forward and up, to allow the whole body to lengthen and widen'.

Reflecting on his early days of training, an actor said:

The actor is better equipped for performance if he has a sound working knowledge of his anatomy and physiology. It is important that the actor understands how the body functions and coordinates in action. An awareness of the skeletal system enables him to consider all the joints for flexibility and range in movement. A basic knowledge of the muscles helps to understand strength. In the real world, nobody admires someone who is slouching, in terms of whether you are talking to them or engaging with them. Therefore, as a tool for a person out in the world, it is invaluable in terms of interaction or presenting yourself as a positive individual with a physical presence and composure in a social situation. Alexander Technique is like looking through the rear-view mirror when you are driving: it is just a glance but it is a way to check on yourself. When I pass by a shop window and I look at myself and see that I am totally off-balance, I now know how to move myself up and improve instantly. Sometimes, I'll spy myself in a mirror and I 'm pleasantly surprised: gee, I'm not too bad with a little straightening here and there. Overall I'm way better, I'm not slouching as much. I used to think of myself as 5'11"; now I'm more than 6' tall. I enjoy being tall and seeing the world at my full height. I am appreciating moving through life as a big person. I was never comfortable with being a big person, I wanted to be a medium size, so I would close my body in, hunch forward and concave myself. But that doesn't happen any more as I have more awareness and it just feels better. If you feel bad, it is just a matter of minutes to simply sit down and be thinking about your body, taking inventory and focusing on the head / neck and breathing and relaxing.

Every actor should study anatomy books to learn about the muscles and the bones. Detailed drawings of the anatomy are exquisite and a fascinating study of design and function. The more the actor knows about his physical instrument and the magnificence of the body's design, the more he will enhance his clarity of thinking when he attempts to use and challenge himself in movement. The basic musculo-skeletal system drawings I have used here come from a wonderful anatomy book, *The Body Moveable* by David Gorman, published by Ampersand Press. You can study many more detailed drawings of this reference book at www.learningmethods.com/ampersand.htm

The Actor Prepares – Warming Up

Preparing the Actor for Rehearsal or Performance

Having been introduced to the Alexander principles and some basic anatomy, you can begin to analyse movement. Watch footage of Olympic racers to note how runners move easily, the muscles of the legs have length and lovely extension, one can always observe forward motion. Watch the runner fire out of the starting gate and you will see the head shoot forward and upward, connecting the power from their back and legs. Take any athlete and you will see the primary control principle of movement. Consider the diver preparing to perform an inward dive in a pike position, the head directing forward and upward to touch the toes, sending the bottom up through space, acting as a fulcrum in the movement. The next time you see a sporting event, watch the slow-motion replay and you will be able to analyse the action by observing the head-neck-back relationship. You will see Alexander's principle in action in most of the players. We could expand on each and every sport: hockey, soccer, basketball, equestrian, track and field, and discuss the coordination of every athlete from an Alexander point of view.

In this next section, we will look at the actor's warm-up. The warm-up is a means of preparing the body for a rehearsal or for the run of a show. The warm-up is not a 'workout'. A workout is the actor's pursuit of fitness and strength-building for the body. Working out may be aerobic exercise, weight training, Pilates classes or any sport. However, the warm-up is a gentle procedure of connecting breath and movement to engage the actor's body into a state of readiness to act. The goal of a warm-up is to open the joints, and to free the musculature through a series of specific extensions and contractions of the muscles and joints as a way of waking and alerting the body to the possibilities of movement.

Let's begin to observe and experiment with our own bodies in movement. Please proceed only if you are free of chronic pain or injury. A note of caution to the novice who has had no physical training: you do not have the benefit of an Alexander teacher or a movement expert's outside eye observing how you are performing the exercises. Only you can know your own body and your physical history and therefore you must judge your own ability. Try these exercises. They are not strenuous, but do listen to your body for feedback and stop if you are experiencing any discomfort or pain. These exercises are not the Alexander Technique, however, they have evolved from my Alexander knowledge and personal experience of warming up the actor.

To experience the benefit of the following series of exercises, one must experiment through performing them. It is virtually impossible to accomplish this while reading this book, as one's attention is actively involved in reading. It might be beneficial for the reader to read the instructions into a tape recorder. When recording, read slowly, breathe and allow enough time to perform the exercises, and leave time for a pause and transition time between the exercises. Perhaps it would be helpful to engage a partner to read the text in order to allow you to go through the movement process. The actor must be free to get down on the floor and follow the sequence of instructions and allow the body to explore the directions of the given exercise. Give yourself enough time to think and breathe through the exercise to allow your body to release the muscles and free the joints. Time is a luxury you must afford to explore this work safely and successfully. The entire warm-up sequence should take the actor about fifteen to twenty minutes to perform.

Warm-up Exercises

1. Stretching on the Mat – Lying on the Back in the Semi-supine Position

- Let's begin with lying down on your back, face up, on a mat or rug on the floor.

- Allow yourself to relax for a minute to let your awareness drop into the body.
- Let the legs lengthen out along the floor. Notice where the body makes contact with the floor.
- Observe the 'topography' of the shape of the body as it receives support from the floor.
- Breathe into the extremities of the hands and toes.
- Extend and release these extremities. Imagine creating space in all the joints.
- Allow the knees to flop open and away from one another. Ask the ankles to slide along the floor, moving your feet towards your bottom. Now turn the feet over and on to the floor, thereby directing the knees upwards towards the ceiling.
- Your heels should be lined up with the sit bones which gives the torso a fairly square and open position on the floor. This is called the 'semi-supine position'.
- Think out of the top of the head. You may use the image of a beam of light shining out of the 'baby's soft spot' at the top of the crown, in the centre of the head.
- Draw both knees up, resting your hands on your knee caps. I call this the 'powder me, diaper me position'.
- Breathe and encourage the thighs to stretch towards the chest. Lightly pulsate the movement.
- You will feel the sit bones move off and away from the mat, towards the direction of the knees.
- Imagine the sit bones as separating or opening away from each other. This is the pelvic floor.
- Take a moment to allow for breath and release in this area.
- Decrease the pull on the knees, but maintain the elevation of the legs.
- Direct the sit bones to release and travel back to the floor while maintaining some stretch in the legs. This movement allows for the counter-flexion of the sacrum and the lower back.
- Once again, draw the knees up by grasping the back of the thighs. Gently rock your pelvis by rolling the knees in a circular motion. Be sure to circle the knees around and around in both directions.
- Consider the butterfly shape of the pelvis, noticing the sit bones at

the base of the pelvis and observing how you have pulled them off the mat towards the direction of the knees. While maintaining a gentle pull of the thighs, allow the sit bones to release and return back to the floor.

* Let your feet and calves spring up towards the ceiling, which will stretch the whole leg. Release at the knees and then repeat the springing action in the legs playfully. Stretch the legs up towards the ceiling, sustaining the stretch for a few moments, and then release at the knee again.
* Place one foot at a time back on the floor, in the semi-supine position. Let each leg lengthen out along the floor, one at a time.
* Let the legs relax. Roll the ankles in and out. Release.
* Initiate a light kicking and vibration of the legs on the floor, as if having a mild temper tantrum. Just let the leg muscles jiggle and shake. They will be bouncing slightly off the floor.
* Release and breathe, to enhance relaxation.

2. Engaging the Abdominal Wall and the Back Muscles

* Direct your legs into the semi-supine position.
* While on your back in the semi-supine position, breathe and observe the contact that the torso is making with the floor. There is a natural curvature in the spine; there is no need to push your back muscles into the floor. The spine will lengthen during this exercise.
* Notice the contact your feet have on the floor.
* Press the feet into the mat while encouraging the lower body to elevate off the mat. Initiate this movement by elevating the pubic bone upwards. At the same time, direct the knees and legs to lengthen towards the ceiling.
* Both the abdominal and the thigh muscles will engage as the body is making a 45-degree angle. The upper back and the shoulders are still on the floor. Your bottom and thighs are elevated about five or six inches off the floor.
* Pause in this position and breathe into the back ribs behind the engaged abdominal wall.
* Now, slowly allow the whole pelvis structure to release and drop

downwards, to hang like a hammock about an inch off the floor.

- Lightly, let the lower body reunite with the floor by simply letting the body gently sink back on to the floor. Notice if the lower body naturally moves towards the head.
- Has the body's contact with the floor changed?
- Does the upper thorax feel congested and do you sense a need to lengthen the upper back? Go ahead and shift the ribs and shoulders of the upper back towards the head.
- The neck will now feel contracted. Allow your fingers to travel to the back of the skull. Stay off the neck muscles and simply support the weight of the skull.
- Let the wrists and fingers relax.
- Consider how the occipital joint (the top of the spine) is located directly behind the uvula at the back of your throat.
- Initiate and support the movement of the head to curl forward from the occipital joint. Let the head move to the point of being able to look between the knees.
- You will feel a stretch of the *trapezius*, the neck muscles. This stretch is originating from the mid back, between the shoulder blades, where the neck muscles insert at the ribcage. (See the diagram in the Anatomy Lesson section.)
- Breathe into the back and into the ribs.
- Support the weight of the head while returning the skull back to the floor.
- Take the hands away. Notice the contact your torso is making with the floor. Has there been a change? Is the body in more contact with the floor?
- Repeat this entire process from the beginning.
- The body should now be in a neutral prone position. The abdominal wall lengthens from the pubic bone. All the back muscles (the *latissimus dorsi*) should be uniformly organized in the same direction. Should you wish to proceed into abdominal exercises such as sit- ups or tummy crunches, you are ready and organized to do so. Remember to repeat this exercise after any abdominal workout in order to return to neutral.

3. A Shoulder Stretch

- Remain in the semi-supine position.
- Initiate movement of both arms by allowing the fingers to float up towards the ceiling.
- Jiggle your hands to flex all the joints in the fingers and the wrists.
  - Let the backs of your arms shake like jelly.
- Press the palms up towards the ceiling and enjoy that stretch. Release.
- While maintaining a release in the joints, gently move the arms around in space.
- Keep the arms extending upwards, as if drawing a direct line from the shoulders up towards the hands.
- Allow one hand to travel over to the other wrist and gently pull the arm directly up towards the ceiling and release. Try not to cross the arm diagonally over the chest.
- You will feel an opening action of the shoulder blade around the ribs as it lifts off the floor. Now decrease the pull at the wrist and let the shoulder return to the floor while maintaining an easy stretch of the arm.
- Welcome the extension and the natural contraction of the stretching muscles of the arm.
- Release both shoulders and repeat the gentle pull of the opposite arm.
- Maintain both arms in an upward extension and simply give both arms a playful shake.
- Elongate through the fingers and take the longest route to cross the arms over each other, giving yourself a warm embrace.
- You should feel the shoulder blades open up. Leave space between the chest and the upper arms. There is no need to squeeze tightly.
- Allow the breath to drop into the back, filling with the expanse of the ribcage. Let the arms open up and release into neutral at the sides of the body.

4. Getting Up Off the Floor

- Place yourself in the semi-supine position, making sure your heels line up with the sit bones.

- Direct your knees up towards the ceiling. Let the thigh muscles lengthen as the knees flop over to one side.
- Continue to think of lengthening the muscles towards the knees and you will feel more of a stretch along the top leg. Breathe.
- Do you sense the diagonal stretch along the intercostal muscles of your ribs and waistline? Breathe into the swing of the ribs and the opening of the side of the body.
- To initiate the return, direct your knees away from the torso as the legs swing back into the semi-supine position.
- Allow the knees to direct upwards as they flop over to the other side. Is this side less flexible than the other? Breathe into the diagonal stretch of the muscles.
- Return to the semi-supine position by initiating lengthening through the thighs towards the knees. Relax for a moment.
- Release your knees over and on to your preferred side. Let your arms and body follow the lead of your legs. You should find yourself in a lengthened foetal position.
- Lead by sending your head away from your body and press your hands into the floor, taking the upper-body weight into your arms. Let your hips swing up off the floor so that you are now on your knees.
- Step one foot forward between your hands and let the back foot rock on to the toes.
- Step the back foot forward. Breathe as you gently unroll the 'C' curvature of the spine, leaving the head to come up last. See out into the space.
- Release the front of the ankles. Observe the hint of a forward sensation in the body.

5. Finding Balance or 'Centre'

- Begin in an open standing position. Place your feet about ten to twelve inches apart, the toes facing forwards.
- Adjust your feet so that the ankle joints line up below the sit bones.
- Playfully rock the weight of your body forwards and then backwards.
- You will feel off balance as you transfer your weight from resting

solely in your heels to solely on the balls of the feet. Notice how you gain balance when you allow the dispersal of your weight to distribute over the whole foot.

● Soften the tendons at the front of the ankles to release the ankle joints. Do you sense a release in the knees?

● Allow the distribution of your weight to spread over the entire arch of the foot. Allow pressure to spread on to the front of the foot (the metatarsal), to sense the breadth and width of the toes and balls of the feet while at the same time maintaining contact in the heels.

● Contact with the floor will help engage our anti-gravity reflexes to lengthen up through the spine.

● Breathe to release and soften the sternum (the breastbone). You will feel movement in your back ribs. Think of the three-dimensional ribcage to enliven the full circumference of the torso and the limbs.

● The discs are located between the vertebrae and towards the front of the spinal column. They act as shock absorbers. (See the Anatomy Lesson section for a diagram reference.)

● An emphasis on a forward direction is found in all movement. The test for this forward equilibrium is whether, when standing in neutral, one can gently be pushed off balance. Allow someone to push you gently and you will immediately feel your whole body moving forward to maintain balance and composure.

● If your leg joints are released and you have a forward poise through the torso, you will be centred and ready to move in any direction.

6. Arm Stretching

● Standing in your neutral, 'centred' stance, think of raising your arms above your head but do not move them.

● Where do you feel the impulse to initiate raising your arms? Do you sense the need to lift from the outer upper-arm muscles? Do you elevate your shoulder blades? Inhibit your initial impulse by pausing and not acting on it.

● Instead, wiggle your fingers, letting all the joints in your hands be free and open.

● Initiate the movement from the fingers to raise one of your arms and as the arm follows the fingers, allow the wrists to be fluid and the elbows free.

- Remembering your anatomy, let the muscles of the arm engage incrementally. Notice the connection of the upper-arm muscles to the *latissimus dorsi* (the back muscles) and the pectoral muscles (the chest muscles). Look at the anatomy diagrams if you need to visualize these muscles.
- Avoid lifting the shoulder blades.
- Think of the support for the weight of the arm as coming up from the lower body.
- Release the sternum and breathe.
- Allow the muscles in your arms to stretch by extending in two directions, both up and down, like an elastic band. There is no need to overstretch.
- Release the front of your ankles.
- Now engage the fingers of the opposite arm and allow the arm muscles to lengthen and widen upwardly to join the other arm.
- With both arms extending over your head, let the fingers of the first arm reach further up. Do you sense the intercostal muscles (the diagonal rib muscles) kick in and extend through the torso? Release the reaching but keep upholding the arm.
- Soften the sternum. Let your arms hang upwardly in space.
- Repeat this by engaging the opposite arm into an extended reach. Observe which muscles are recruited to stretch this arm.
- Wave both arms about. Let all the joints be supple. Are you experiencing any fatigue in the arms? If you are, think of your lower body coming up off the hip joints to help support the weight of the arms. Breathe.
- Release the arm by bending at the elbow and be careful not to collapse your torso with the action of releasing the weight of the arm. Release the other arm.
- Gently shake out the arm muscles.
- Again, lengthening the fingers in both hands and opening the joints, extend both arms outwards from the shoulder in a 'T' formation.
- Think of widening the *latissimus dorsi* muscles in the back and the pectoral muscles across the front of the torso to support the arms. Allow for open space in the underside of the ball-and-socket joint,

deep in the armpit. Notice the engagement of those big torso muscles and how they attach into the inner-upper arms.

- Let the ribs enjoy the open space by breathing.
- Release the arms again and observe if you sense more freedom in the shoulder area and in your ribcage.
- Elevate your arms so that your hands are palms down, directly in front of you, no higher than your shoulders. Rotate your hands over and over and over again.
- Now ask the question, do my hands rotate on the axis of my thumbs or on the axis of my baby fingers? Repeat the movement and find out the answer.
- The design of the two bones of the forearms makes it is easier to rotate the hands on the axis of the baby finger. Notice when you rotate on the axis of the thumbs you will sense a slight strain in the musculature. Now, think of lengthening along the axis of the baby finger and you should observe more freedom and ease in the rotation. It helps to enhance the connection of the back and chest muscles to support the movement of the arm.
- Thinking of lengthening the arm along the line of the baby finger is useful for lifting heavy objects, extending to reach for an object, playing the piano and simply elevating your arms over your head.

7. Undulating Through Centre

- Keep your eyes open, to enable yourself to see up and out into the studio.
- Touch the breastbone and explore how the ribs come into the sternum and then trace them out, individually. You may find that there is tenderness in places. Just apply a gentle pressure for stimulus. It is common to find tension stashed between those ribs.
- Gently release the legs by softening the knees and ankles.
- We are playing with the potential for flexion of the ribcage and the spine.
- Put one hand on the back and one on the sternum and explore your flexibility with an undulation and movement of your ribs. Your ribs can move from side to side and up and down.
- One has to move right through the pelvis and up through the neck

to increase the range of movement. The movement is now an undu-
lating wave from head to toe, not from side to side.

- Renew the release in your ankles and relax your arms.
- Stretch up through the torso when you bend to one side. Breathe in
and out to sense the movement of the ribs several times. Do not
rush your breath. Go at your own pace.
- Repeat the stretch on the other side. Enjoy the stretch of the intercostal muscles that diagonally intersect the shape of the ribcage.
- Rest both hands around the ribs above the waist. Observe the action
or movement of simply breathing. Notice how you can sense the
movement in the full circumference of the ribcage.
- Let your hands release. Observe the energy in your hands. Whenever
one does some massaging of the body, one will feel some energy
absorbed by the hands. Shaking or later washing the hands will
clear that energy away.

8. Find the Hip Joint

- To find the great trocanter, which is the bone of the leg and hip joint,
refer to the Anatomy Lesson diagrams in the previous section. Let
the arms relax at the side of the torso. Now press the heel of the
palms into the sides of the legs.
- Release the knees.
- The palms should make contact with a bony protruding shape. This
is the great trocanter, which is the exterior end of the ball-and-
socket joint. Most people will find the hip joint this way. However,
some people may have very long arms which will extend further
down the leg.
- When you bend the knees, you will feel the action of movement in
the hips in your palms.
- Observe how the sit bones travel back as the upper body moves
slightly forward.
- Swing your hips into your hands, creating a circular motion. Let the
pubic bone and the sit bones circle in both directions. I call this the
'dirty dog school of dancing'.
- Think of the whole torso moving upwardly, off the hip joints.
Notice the potential to rock and roll at this juncture of the body.

The hip joints are the largest joints in the body and we neglect to use them enough.

- Freedom to move in the hip joints promotes any extended stretch in the legs and in the upper torso.
- Keep your feet in contact with the floor and release all your joints into movement.
- Allow the whole body to undulate, including your head, neck, shoulders and torso.
- Release all the joints and move. We shall see some wonderful shapes and configurations. Go on, release the joints and go for it with gay abandon!

9. The Rolling-over Exercise

Everyone has attempted the seemingly simple task of touching one's toes. How many fitness classes, workout routines and actor warm-ups include this activity? Many individuals are challenged and dismayed by their inflexibility and inability to reach over to make that all-important contact with the toes. When asked to analyse or describe this movement, the response is one of 'Gosh, I simply flop over, I don't think about it.'

By engaging one's thinking and following a sequential direction to organize the musculo-skeletal system, it is possible to accomplish or improve this activity.

- Assume an open stance, with your feet apart.
- Point the toes forward.
- The ankles should be in a line, below the sit bones.
- Soften the tendons at the front of the ankles and release the knees slightly.
- What is your initial response to the idea of rolling over? Do you drop your body downwards when you want to flop over?
- Inhibit the flopping-over impulse.
- Be aware of your three-dimensional head and see up and out into the room.
- Gently initiate moving the head from the top of the spine at the occipital joint, which is located directly behind the uvula.

- By simply allowing the nose to tilt forward, one will be looking at the floor.
- Notice how that movement begins a stretch in the neck muscles. The origin of the neck muscle comes up from between the shoulder blades.
- The emphasis and direction of this entire rolling-over movement is upwards.
- Do not rush downwards towards the floor.
- Continue to roll forward, allowing the breastbone to travel upwardly and towards the spine as the shoulder girdle and arms release forwards.
- Allow the 'C' curvature to take shape in your chest.
- Breathe.
- Check your knees and ankles maintain a mild flexion in the joints.
- Imagine the navel or belly button as travelling up towards the ceiling, creating the shape of a large 'C' curve.
- Now think of the pubic bone as heading upwards.
- Counter any sense of falling forwards with increased flexion in the knees and ankles.
- It may help to think of the knees as opening and bending away from each other, directing them over the ankle joints.
- Allow time to pause and breathe in this position.
- Notice how your bottom ribs swing with the breathing.
- Have the intention of the sit bones opening as if separating from one another. Smile at your neighbour!
- Let the joints and the muscles in the arms relax.

Your head should be hanging freely off the top of the spine and dangling towards the floor. Your point of view will be looking between the legs.

- Keep the eyes active and open, despite the limited, upside-down perspective.
- When you are ready to return to an upright stance, carefully initiate the movement by thinking of the pubic bone moving towards the ceiling. This will encourage the sit bones to point towards the heels once again.
- Think of unfolding slowly and incrementally, maintaining the 'C' shape, and again have the intention that your navel is directing up

towards the ceiling.
- Then direct the breastbone upwardly as you unroll the spine, slowly allowing each vertebrae to float up towards the ceiling.
- Your point of view is still towards the floor.
- Leave the head until the end of the movement and simply ask your eyes to look out into the room and your head will move upright.
- You may feel the urge to adjust the shoulders or pull them back, or hoist your chest to straighten up. Don't. Inhibit the urge to adjust yourself, because that is an old, habitual impulse. A shoulder adjustment will simply negate the benefits of rolling over.
- Allow a forward sensation through the shoulders. Take note of how the body is organized. Does your whole body feel tilted forward?
- Could the body be easily pushed off balance? Do you sense a state of readiness?
- Do you have a sense of the volume and dimension of the torso?
- Breathe, and again release the joints in the legs.
- The forward sensation one experiences is a result of bringing the weight of the body forwards on to the front of the spine where the discs are housed, thus permitting the discs to do the job of support and shock absorption.
- Observe these unfamiliar sensations without any readjusting and shaking. Old habits will return soon enough.
- Walk around the room and then repeat the exercise to detect whether your flexibility and range of bending over has increased.
- This forward sensation of your weight and the spine increases flexibility or what I call the 'oingo boingo' in movement.
- Can you now understand the purpose of the exercise of rolling over in voice class, or movement class?
- Are you able to observe the forward sensation that the action of rolling over has created in the body? When the weight and balance of the body is organized towards the front of the spine, it allows the body more access to the shock-absorbing function of the discs. This improves the quality of the movement as it reduces stress and downward pressure in the spine.
- I would argue that upon analysis of the elements in a fitness regime or stretching routine, one will discover that one moves without constructive thought or mindfulness. The Alexander Technique is

thinking in action. Thinking of freeing the neck, to allow the spine to lengthen, is a direction that will enhance performance and reduce extraneous tension.

10. Balancing into Walking

- Find a neutral, open stance.
- Stand on one leg. Remember to think up and off the hip joint. If you feel off balance, hold on to the side of a table.
- Shake the free leg loosely from the hip joint as if shaking yesterday's underwear out of your jeans.
- Let the leg hang and swing freely.
- Slowly and gently, allow the foot to release back on to the floor and sense how the foot widens and spreads out.
- Notice how the weight of the upper body moves forward from the hip joint right over that leg as the foot makes contact with the floor.
- Change legs, no doubt to the less-preferred leg.
- Lightly shake the muscles to loosen the other leg. It needn't be taut or controlled. Let it loosen like a 'drunken sailor's leg'.
- Again, as one gently allows the foot to release on to the floor, observe how the body moves forward and upwards over the foot.
- As you release the leg, allow the placement of the foot to widen and spread out upon contact with the floor. You will notice that the body needs to move over the foot and leg.
- The whole body propels into forward motion. This is the beginning of walking. As we think of the body moving in a forward and upward direction, we can move up out of the hip joints, thereby freeing the legs to move easily.
- Go walking about the room and do not over-stride. Your body should be over your feet. Do you tend to walk by leading with your feet ahead of your body? Many of you will need to shorten your stride. The forward sensation in your walking will seem foreign because it is not your habit.
- Stop and rest. Do you want to drop down into your hip joints?
- Walk backwards about the space. Do you become more aware of your whole back? As you step backwards, think of your whole body as moving forward and upwards. Keep your feet under you. •

Do you feel alive in your back?

● Now try moving in all directions, while maintaining a forward direction in the body and thinking up and off your legs. Do the cha-cha.

● See how freely you can change direction by thinking of the whole body with an upward intention. Bravo!

11. An Open-leg Stretch

● Open the legs and feet to take a comfortable yet wider stance. Your feet should be further apart than your shoulder width. Some will know this as second position in dance.

● Soften the front of the ankles.

● While bending the backs of the knees, think of directing the knees away from each other.

● Release the knees forward over the ankles and toes, in what I call the 'samurai warrior' stretch. The toes can either be squared or slightly turned out. The body remains upright.

● While bending, imagine the sit bones separating as if opening away from one another. We want to release the extra tension and clenching in all those pelvic-floor muscles, i.e. the perineum and the sphincter.

● Breath will encourage relaxation and release in this centre position.

● While maintaining the depth, move from the centre position by lengthening through the torso as you shift the whole body over one leg. Do not let the knee bend past the toes. Maintain a right angle alignment of the knee and toe.

● As you shift your body over the leg, have an upward intention in the movement. Direct the butterfly-shaped pelvic bone up towards the ceiling when extending over the bent leg and knee.

● The upward direction opens the stretch by releasing any downward compression in the hip joint.

● A maximum stretch is achieved by simply shifting one's weight forward over the legs. Further enhance the stretch by directing your head away from the body to lengthen the spine.

● An emphasis on allowing the skeleton to move engages the muscles easily, thereby avoiding overstretching and pulling on the musculature.

- The muscles in the body respond to gentle encouragement and rebel against force.
- You may feel this tomorrow in your bottom and legs, but not in a punitive way.
- Shake one leg at a time, allowing the foot to gently recontact the floor.
- Walk into and around the room and take notice of the quality of your movement. Do you sense an increased lightness in your walking? Consider other warm-up stretches that you use. Could the Alexander thought process be applied to them?
- Now for the important question. Are you warmed up and ready to act?

PART 2

Putting the Alexander Technique to Work

Partner Work – Moving in Relationship

Having suggested a few warm-up exercises in the last chapter, we shall now prepare to experiment with more rigorous partnered movement work. We have gone through a basic warm-up for the body and we should be ready to move. The Alexander work is the root and core of my personal exploration of movement. I want to be clear in stating that these exercises are examples of the application of the Alexander Technique to movement work and not the Alexander Technique per se.

Later in this section, I shall provide a description of Alexander's table work. A lesson in the table work must be experienced with a trained Alexander Technique teacher in order to truly benefit the student. The trained hands-on technique of the teacher will stimulate a freedom and openness in the body. The student needs to have the kinesthetic experience of the teacher's guidance in order to understand authentically the physical changes that occur in the Alexander lesson.

Now, let's go further into movement work, beginning with spatial awareness exercises and progressing into partnered contact improvisation.

Partner Work and Spatial Awareness Exercises

It is important that the actor should have a sense of his three-dimensional, voluminous body. We tend to be frontal in our awareness of our physical selves, forgetting our backs and the full circumference of our limbs and torso. Are you familiar with the Leonardo da Vinci drawing of a man with his arms outstretched, showing the dimensions and symmetry of the body? This demonstrates that the span of a man's arms, his diameter, is equal to his height.

Asking the actor to claim his three-dimensional diameter in space heightens his animal or creature awareness. One can immediately sense the presence of another being if and when they move within the range or sphere of one's diameter. When one actor approaches the other from the back, the actor's presence will be felt as soon as they step into the kinespherical diameter of the other actor's height and width. We've all had the discomforting experience of a person who lacks spatial awareness being 'in your face' or not 'respecting your space'. When one recoils or moves back from the confrontation, it is a physical and animal response.

On a more positive note, everyone has had the experience of 'having a crush', or being attracted to someone at a party. When that person is not in your line of vision, you can still sense where they are in the room and with whom they are talking. Should that special person change location in the room, we seem to have radar which knows where they are in the space. All this information is registering without actually having to turn around and look directly at them. How is it that we can observe the 'other' in this way? We do not have eyes in the back of our heads. I believe that our creature cognition has engaged to heighten our senses. When one is fully engaged in the body, it enhances the awareness of being in space. The body has a sense of a depth of field in relation to others which allows our perception to increase. We are 'turned on'. When a person becomes aware of the full volume of energy in the body, they achieve a clearer sense of the limbs gesturing in space. They become less frontal and gain a stronger sense of the back. Here are some spatial awareness exercises to explore with a group of warmed-up actors. This exercise requires a room that is large enough to house actors in movement.

1. Spatial Awareness Exercises

Interactive Spatial Exercise with a Partner

- Stand erect and elevate your arms to observe the expanse of your arms. That expanse is approximately the extent of your height. You are about as wide as you are tall.
- To get a sense of your 5'2" or 6'1" diameter, stretch your limbs and

reach around you. Extend your arms around in front, behind and above you to establish how much space you fill or require for your body's size and the diameter of your dimensions.

- Release your arms and see out into the room.
- While remembering the space of your diameter, move about the room and take up and fill the voluminous space of your body's diameter.
- Do you notice when another actor has intersected your personal diameter?
- Observe how the entire space of the room is being utilized.
  Choose a partner and establish who is A and who is B.
- The As should then experiment with moving in and out of their partner B's personal space or diameter. Be clear in your awareness when you move in and out of the other's kinespherical space.
- Notice how you can sense without touch when someone is within your reach or 'in your space'.
- This exercise heightens the creature sensibility that clearly recognizes when another animal comes within your diameter or kinesphere.
- Play around with partner A moving in and out of partner B's space to allow B to get a sense of depth of field and how much of a diameter or space you require.
- Make your partner feel your presence. Do not touch them, but do confront or even crowd them.
- Do you stop breathing when you confront your partner? Does your breath change?
- Remember to breathe while moving and confronting the other.
- Explore the entering and the exiting energy that you put off as you move through the partner's space.
- You don't need eyes in the back of your head to see or sense someone behind you. We have a kinesthetic sense of depth of field.
- Explore the subtle sensitivity of knowing when you are in and out of the diameter of your partner.
- Try not to talk in these exercises. Rely on your senses to communicate.
- Switch roles, allowing the Bs to lead the exercise. Allow yourself to respond. There is no need to be static.
- Take up the space that is all around you.

- Let your peripheral vision see out into the room.
- Are you tuning in to your partner? Is the energy exchange between you stimulated? Are your senses tuning up?
- What information does that give you about them? It is likely that your sense of where you are in space is heightened because someone is moving into your space.
- Enjoy playing with the magnetic field of energy you have stimulated with your partner and use the full studio space to stretch and extend that dynamic.
- Exploring your three-dimensional and voluminous body will aid in establishing your energy in the space as well as establishing a dynamic with a partner.
- Pick a new partner. It changes the dynamic immediately, doesn't it?
- As you stand with your new partner, observe how much more you know about your previous partner.
- Do you feel the new partner as a foreign energy?
- Repeat this exercise and see how quickly and expediently you can establish a new dynamic with another actor.

2. Endowment – Observing the Other

What can an actor do when the dynamic with another actor is not happening, when they lack a connection? When faced with this problem, an experienced actor suggests a solution:

Endowment. You have to endow the other actor with everything you think you should be getting and respond like you got it that way. I think of acting like wearing a miner's hat. I'll shine my light on you and you shine yours on me and we each do 50 per cent of the other one's work. Half your job is done by the way I treat you. Then there is a whole bunch of information you won't have to play, and then you do that for me and then we have only 50 per cent of our own part to do. I always look for that connection and if you are not getting it, then you have to receive everything that you are getting as if it was what you needed. This will work for the audience because they will start to see the person as you are seeing them. Actors in an unconscious way can divorce ourselves from somebody we think is not doing a good job and we let the audience in on the idea that they are not so hot, when our job is to make them look as good as possible. The real art of what we do has to be endowment.

Endowment Exercise

- Each actor must choose a partner.
- The partners then observe each other from a comfortable distance, seven or eight feet apart.
- Observe each other within the framework of the space. Look at your partner in relation to the room – the ceiling, the floor, the walls, the windows and door frames. Behold the other in relation to the depth of field the partner's body has to furniture, other classmates, the pictures on the walls, etc.
- The observed actor will sense the attention coming from their partner.
- Endowing the other 's presence in the space observable is a simple way to heighten the actor's three-dimensional awareness of the other player.
- Recall how one savours the physical details of a love interest. You know the experience of feeling a private ownership or claim to a physical characteristic of a lover, how the corner of the loved one's smile is yours and yours alone. The way a romantic love interest rolls their eyes or wets their lips becomes a personal private asset.
- Notice eight details about your partner: an arch in the eyebrow, a mole on the neck, a dimple in the cheek, the turnout of a leg, the shape of the shoulder, the colour of the shoes, the length of hair, etc.
- Begin to move around each other and, while moving, continue to observe your partner in a changing framework or point of view. Note how the relationship to walls and furniture changes, the reflection of light, the changing background, while observing the three-dimensional body moving in the space.
- When moving, continue to observe those eight details that heightened your curiosity and perception of the other.
- Choose one distinct physical detail. Hold that in your mind as a special secret.

- Move apart and away from your partner. Find your own private space in the room.
- Recall the image of your partner. Imagine all those details that you observed, especially that one special detail.
- Turn and move towards a reunion with your partner.
- As the other comes back into your view, find pleasure in clocking that one special secret detail.
- Circle each other.
- Note if you sense a heightened sensibility between you and your partner.

3. Stage 2 of Spatial Awareness

The next step to take is to move into the kinespherical field of your partner. Let's interrelate to where you are within the range of touching each other.

- Do not touch, but begin to move, circling around each other within this more intimate, interactive field.
- Observe your breath. Are you breathing? Has the closeness of your partner changed your breathing?
- The movement heightens the awareness of each other in space and stirs up a magnetic field of energy. You are beginning to establish the chemistry of the partnership.
- The depth of field is relative to the size and dimension of the skeletal structure of the body. The energy exchange is the live animal factor.
- The next step allows one partner to make physical contact by simply touching the other.
- It is important for the actor to initiate contact by sensing the beginning, the middle and the finishing of that physical contact. Our sensitivity heightens by moving through and filling the space as we make an initial contact.
- Once contact is made, there is a message exchanged between players. The contact has palpable, observable kinesthetic qualities. There is information about your partner. A communication of

'giving' and 'getting' comes into play.

- Explore moving in and out of each other's space and, one by one, initiate a touch. Allow each other to answer with a responsive touch and carry on a dialogue that is kinesthetic and non-verbal. A story will evolve between the players.

This exercise will prove invaluable on the stage. When the actor heightens his physical presence and creature energy in his interactive relationships, the audience will feel a dynamic between the players. We call it having a 'chemistry' when the actors are physically attentive and focused on one another. This exercise also helps the actor to understand that interaction and physical contact must not be general or it will lack communication and theatricality. The Alexander Technique can help the actor to gain physical awareness and consciousness of the three-dimensional body. Interacting with another actor takes the Alexander work into action.

Our animal territorial awareness of space is very important to know and to establish on stage. For example, when staging a scene between the Montagues and Capulets, who within the crowd of Italian characters are the star-crossed lovers? The audience needs to be aware of Romeo and Juliet by their heightened and focused dynamic. Perhaps the designer has worked peach and silver into both their costumes to illustrate their connection, but it is the actors' chemistry that will tell the story.

When asked what they learn in the spatial awareness classes, a few young actors expressed their response:

I learned that the trick to having an actor's presence is to recognize where your space exists. I like to command a large space and with that awareness, when your body comes alive, the space around your body becomes alive too. When your body is turned on, you have a certain understanding of the space behind you, it helps in sensing and gauging how much space you have. There is that awareness of other actors when you feel their energy, it is an energy that starts to feed itself with another actor when you are on stage. When performing with that space and when those energies collide, there immediately emerges either a comfortable or a conflicted relationship. When the tension occurs, it is great and becomes interesting to watch. Alexander teaches an awareness of your body. It is such an invaluable tool to have an awareness of the space in and around your body, as it helps to create your world and how you exist in it. You can play 'It's my space, so don't piss me off', or 'Welcome into my space'. Alexander work is a tool that you can use every day as a personal strengthening device to affect your presence and how people perceive you.

In my training with the Alexander work, the emphasis on spatial awareness has helped me to realize the space I have on stage. Thinking up helps me to be balanced. I am able to make an entrance on stage and walk down the stairs without having to look down at the stairs. It helps me to move on stage safely. You have to keep reminding yourself, since you have all these physical habits that come back. I have the habit of sitting down into my hips and then I shoot my legs out forward, making my presence seem low and sunken into the ground. I need to constantly remind myself to lift out of my hips and to shorten my steps so that my stride is more balanced. When I sense my legs underneath me, I appear more graceful and I feel more in control. I've enjoyed the experiment of being at a party and while talking with some friends I notice a highly attractive, beautiful woman across the room. I begin giving out all those signals from my back. I don't want to look straight at her and be obvious but I want to be alive with my back to attract her. It is great to get a sense of filling your back. For most people, the back is dead, because we tend to think through our eyes at the front of the body.

4. Contact Partner Work.

Always thoroughly warm up the body before moving into any contact partner work. Actors are playful and zealous by nature and therefore must be warned that jumping into partner-movement work can involve some risk to the body. These contact partner exercises should be monitored by a third party with an outside cautionary eye, such as an experienced movement teacher or Alexander teacher. The

Alexander principle of 'non-doing' and allowing the body to move with ease and fluidity helps the actors to avoid overdoing and using tension in the contact. This exercise is a very quick and effective method to jettison physical inhibitions and the polite reservations in a group of actors.

An Introduction to Physical Contact Between Actors

- Organize the group into partnerships of A and B.
- The actors should stand making full-body contact back to back.
- They will observe their skeletons' structural differences: whose shoulders are higher? Where does the body make points of contact? Whose pelvis or bottom is higher or lower? Does one sense the weight and density of the other?
- Can one perceive the other partner's breathing?
- Having observed the back-to-back contact with each other, the actors may move towards and into the point of contact.
- Explore who you are up against. How much range and variation of movement can you allow through the constantly changing, mercurial point of contact? Do you have a sense of their density and proportions?
- As the point of contact changes, so will the dynamic of the physical support of giving and taking with the body. During the course of exploring through movement, the actors will begin to need the partnership to maintain balance and support.
- By ordering the group to freeze, you will find that the partnerships are creating a wild variety of shapes. If one partner were to walk away from the other, they would collapse. The dynamic is symbiotic. It needs both parties to advance and maintain equilibrium. The actors will be able to support each other in movement that would be off balance and impossible to do without the partner. Again, one tunes in to the give and take of the body
- Moving together allows the muscles to stretch and extend. The partner's support will encourage the body to move beyond its normal range of balance and flexibility.
- The actor will learn to take weight and to sustain mobility if the body does not become dead weight. If both parties maintain flexi-

bility and continuous movement, they will roll and tumble together freely. Be mercurial!

● When a partnership finds itself stuck in a shape, they must move towards and into the point of contact because there is always a bit more room to move. The body has a bit of give when one moves into the point of contact.

● The partnerships will now be changing levels and moving about the space in a united fusion of torsos and limbs.

● Return to an upright and neutral stance. Release the contact. The partnership should be back to back but not in contact.

● The actors will observe a warmth or heat in the back which was previously united with their partners, as if they were still connected.

● Move about the room. The actor's intention is to fill and expand into the warm sensation of the back.

● Freeze. Enquire whether the actors are aware of where their partner is located in the space. Most of the actors will instantly find their partner.

● Ask them to turn and see the frontal face of the partner, but have them notice the sense of a warm afterglow of the partners' presence in their backs.

● Think of filling out that voluminous energy as you walk back to reunite with your partner. Fall back into the exercise and renew contact with your partner.

● Continue to play with the partnership dynamic and the point of contact. While moving, see up and out, keeping the eyes open. It is important to know where one is in space. The dynamic of the partnership builds trust.

● This exercise helps to bring out the bear cub in an actor: getting them to play, using the body and not the brains when creating a dynamic with another. It is, happily, an anti-intellectual process.

● One must take time to explore and familiarize oneself with another creature's energy. This is an unique form of dialogue. Taking the time to communicate and expressing oneself through the body with another actor is the name of the game.

● Come back to your autonomy and stand beside your partner.

● Proudly walk about the space with your partner. Show off your alliance and interact with other partnerships.

- Change partners. Clear the slate of any preconceived ideas about the new partner: you cannot tell a body by its cover. Repeat but do not rush the process. It take time to read the new partner.
- Experiment with listening and receiving information through the back and the body.
- Observe the breath of the new partner. Does their back give you a sense of density and proportion?
- How susceptible and yielding are you with the new partner? The notion of giving in order to get something is a key element of making the exercise move forward.
- After five to ten minutes, separate and turn face to face, to observe the partner.
- Take pleasure in moving about the space with your partner. You will be surprised to learn how much insight and familiarity has been established in this new partnership.

This is a great game for the early stages of rehearsal or the onset of a movement course as it will liberate the group from self-conscious inhibitions and intellectual dynamics. Recalling his movement training in theatre school, an actor explains:

> In the early days of my movement training, we did a good deal of work on the mat in partners. It was a great acting exercise because you would have to let go of your own inhibitions. There you would be, rolling all over everybody, your bottom in someone's face and their knees in yours. You simply could not be polite about it. When you let things go and don't think about it, then the Alexander principle is inherent in the movement. By instinct, you keep moving and use the other person's weight or you give them your weight so that nobody gets hurt. It was rigorous, yet surprisingly, nobody overstretched a muscle or hurt their neck or got pinched or trapped in the process. The idea of perpetual movement aids that freedom. I remember your instruction that if you found yourself in a cramped position to keep moving through it and it would work itself out whether the other guy was twice your size or not. The range and variety of movement was amazing. We did some exciting work and learned to trust the others in the group.

Using Contact to Explore Relationships in Rehearsal

In the early days of a rehearsal for *Romeo and Juliet*, the actresses playing Juliet and the Nurse decided that a movement class would be helpful to explore the characters' close and lifelong relationship. Our goal was to provide a private rehearsal for the two women to get to know each other and to break down some formality and inhibitions. These characters must have an intimacy that is relaxed, caring, playful and heartfelt. It is so difficult to play a lifelong relationship with an actor you have never worked with before, and we decided to explore the physical relationship to connect the two characters.

Initially, the two actors worked without language. They began by standing back to back, to learn about each other's height, dimension, density, texture, rhythm and breath. This position liberates the actors from feeling that they have to see into one another's eyes to make a connection. Slowly and gently, they began to move with each other, maintaining some contact with their backs but allowing for a mercurial point of contact. They began to need each other as they explored giving and taking weight from each other. The connection to each other allowed them to make shapes and explore extensions that would have been impossible without the presence and support of the other. The natural play and rhythmic interchange heightened as changes in breath and giggles ensued. I directed them to move on to a couch and wrestle for the better spot, which got them interacting with their entire bodies in a playful and intimate way as each tried to outsmart the other for a better position. This game produced lots of affectionate laughter and physical play between the actors which was true to the relationship of the characters in the play.

We explored embracing and sustaining a supportive contact, even allowing the Nurse to support Juliet's weight and hold her up. Both actresses felt the time was well spent and that, as the characters, they would take a new insight and playfulness back to rehearsal.

When actors are cast as lovers in a play, there needs to be a 'chemistry' between them, informing the audience that the relationship is heightened and special. What is that dynamic and energy that we describe as 'chemistry' on stage? How do the actors evoke it when they have never worked together before, they are in a romantic relationship in their private life, or they are gay, or they don't quite like the actor that has been cast as the love interest? I have often noted in rehearsal, and had feedback from, an actor who is struggling to make a confident connection with their fellow player. Sometimes a scene simply needs a little bit of sexual tension or even a virginal, innocent curiosity. I have worked with many couplings – Romeo and Juliet, Tony and Maria, Hermia and Lysander, Miranda and Ferdinand, Jessica and Lorenzo, Troilus and Cressida – in the rehearsal period. The best way to solve an energy lull in a partnership is to put the actors in corporeal contact, starting back to back. Contact is an expedient way to break down inhibitions and negative blockage between actors. The contact exercises described earlier will take the actors' attention out of the head and intellect and into the physical body. To eliminate language as a communication tool will technically heighten the actor's body language and force the imagination into the physical realm, evoking playfulness and kinesthetic interplay. Having relied solely on their physical relationship to communicate, the actors can later recall the sensory memory and engage the physical dynamic in the scene. One does not have to be intimate with another actor to play intimacy on stage.

5. Centrifugal Force and Opposition Exercises

Step 1 Finding the Whole Back

- With this exercise, you can practise the application of using the whole back. Remember the anatomy of the skeleton. The top of the spine is in the centre of the head and extends all the way down to the sit bones of the pelvic floor.
- Begin by holding on to a sturdy doorknob, a comfortable stride away from the door.
- Proceed by letting the head, the neck and the whole back shift backwards as the arms stretch forward to the doorknob. Try not to contract your neck. Keep the head up and the neck long.
- Allow the sit bones and the upper back to fall backwards while releasing the knees and ankles.

- You will arrive in a squatting position, with your arms stretching up towards the door.
- Hang out there and enjoy the extension of the back muscles. Breathe.
- Send or swing your sit bones further back through space to initiate the momentum to return to an upright position.
- If you are tall, you may want to use the frame of the door jamb if the doorknob is too low.
- Check that the entire length of the back is moving backwards in space.
- Repeat this movement to heighten your awareness of the back moving back in space. Your cautious kinesthetic perception of being off balance will kick in before you actually are off balance. There is more range in your backwards equilibrium than you will normally allow. In the Alexander Technique, this movement is referred to as sending your back back.
- Explore the range of your whole back moving back and then release your knees and ankles.

Step 2 Opposition Exercise -- Stretching in Partnership

- Begin facing a partner.
- Stand with the feet apart. Your feet should be under your torso and in line with the sit bones.
- Join hands with your partner.
- Consider the full length and volume of the torso.
- Begin to allow the back to move away from or in opposition to your partner.
- Your arms will lengthen and stretch forward as the weight of your body moves back through space.
- Make sure that your sit bones are travelling backwards and not tucking in and under.
- Bend the knee and ankle joints.
- Check to see that the upper back is moving with the lower back so that the body is not hunching over. The head/neck and back should be erect and lengthening.
- The weight and opposition of the partner allows you to move back-

wards in space without falling.
- You will be exploring the space behind you that can only be achieved with the support of a partner.
- Challenge the partnership to change levels and explore how opposition gives range and options to the movement.
- If there is any fear of falling back, send the sit bones backwards, which will present the cushioned part of the bottom to the floor.
- Notice that if you direct the energy of your full torso away from your partner, the partnership can move freely upwards and downwards.
- Let all the joints have flexion with the movement. There should be a level of fun and excitement in the room.
- Have the partnership return to a neutral, upright stance.
- The actors will feel the stretch and use of the muscles from this exercise because the partnership heightens and increases the stretch in two directions.
- Did you observe that the movement was enhanced by the power and strength of the whole back? Do you understand the Alexander idea of sending your back back?
- Learning to access and use the whole back is vital for any falling, dancing or combat movement and staging.

Step 3 Centrifugal Force Exercise

- Continue with the same partner. Let's take this opposition stretch a step further. A word of caution, though: this is risky and each actor must take responsibility to say 'stop' if they feel dizzy or out of control.
- Having established a rapport with a partner, you will become familiar with the weight and flexibility of that partner. Begin to explore moving.
- Gradually allow your partnership to start turning by taking small steps and directing the whole back away from the opposite partner.
- Upon finding some momentum, escalate the turning. Keep your steps small and underneath you. See out, despite the spinning!
- Always tell your partner if you have had enough or if you become dizzy.

- The studio will be filled with the excitement of centrifugal force as the partnerships spin rapidly.
- It is great fun to explore the unknown space behind you, relishing the power of the back.
- Some partners will be able to progress from one-handed spinning into releasing one of the partners into a 'tailspin', which is spinning on the bottom and back. This movement recalls a 1980s 'break dancer'.
- Do you recognize a connection of opposition in swing dancing, jive and jitterbug?
- The beauty of a dancing partnership is in the creation of a physical dynamic of space and rhythm. The action of opposition in movement allows for a greater range in the dynamic and enhances the drama of the partnership.
- The space between the partners is where the audience reads a story of chemistry and sexual tension of the dance.
- Switch partners. Be careful to go through all the preliminary steps to acquaint yourself with your new partner. There is risk in this exercise.

6. A Mirroring Exercise

In this classic theatre exercise, we can use the Alexander Technique to observe habits of movement in ourselves and others. Having information as to the primary control and organization of an actor's coordination, we can consider the notion of walking a mile in another man's shoes. Observing habits of movement gives an actor insight into the character. Actors love mimicry and on the strength of a few beers there is no greater amusement than to do a 'piss-take' of another actor's acting. Usually the imitation is a composite of the actor's habit and tension, intensified by the mimic. With the mirroring exercise, the actor will gain awareness of how others observe his movement, his rhythm and, foremost, his identifiable habits. It is painfully informative for a group of actors to learn just how imitative and habitual their movement can be. No actor wants to be identified or recognized by a quirky movement habit when he makes an appearance on stage. The skills of observation and evocation can be vital tools for character acting. Mirroring is a classic theatrical device used in many plays, which will be discussed further in Part 4.

- The mirroring exercise is done in partners, A and B.
- Begin by simply observing the skeletal and muscular organization of the other actor. When observing, ask yourself several questions about the shape and organization of the body of the other.
- What is the relationship of the head to the neck? Does it pull forwards, backwards, or is it tilting to one side?
- Observe where the weight is held. Is the person sitting in one hip more than the other? Is their weight distributed over the front of the foot, or does it seem to be more in the heels?
- Look at the arms in relation to the shoulder and back. Do the hands turn inwards or outwards? Are the fingers open or closed?
- Are the knees locked?
- Do you get a sense of a three-dimensional body?
- Partner A then begins to move around the room, walking, sitting and standing, while partner B moves about with partner A, observing specific details of the body and movement .
- Then partner B begins to allow the detailed observations of partner A to infiltrate and manifest themselves in his own body.
- The point of entry in capturing the 'other' may be a small detail: the swing of an arm, the lead of a foot, the movement of the head, or the drop of a shoulder.
- By allowing the rhythm of this foreign body to move through the actor, partner B is able to capture the manner of use of partnerA.
- Then have partner A fall out to the outskirts of the studio in order for them to observe. The B partner continues moving, evoking the movement of partner A without the immediate visual aid and reference of A.
- There will be lots of giggles as the As observe the partner Bs' renditions of themselves and their inimitable movement.
- PartnerA then re-enters the work space to give B a further opportunity to capture the uniqueness of A's manner.
- Suggest to the As that they allow changes of rhythm, pace, level and direction, giving the Bs more information and challenge.
- Switch roles to allow the As their fair shake at observing and mirroring the movement of their partner B. Repeat the process.

● Change partnerships and have a go with another individual who demonstrates a whole host of habits and idiosyncratic movement.

7. Status Work – Playing the High and the Low Brows

It is important in a drama for the actor to know where the character is positioned in the social hierarchy of his world. Establishing a character's status, be it high or low, will involve the actor's comportment, manners, speech and costuming. The actor will need to embody the character's status in a physical way. The body is the vessel of experience and it will demonstrate whether or not it has power. Drama is a power struggle. The concept of yin and yang can describe the balance of power and shifts in status according to who is driving and dominating a scene. There is a physical component which is observable in the giving and getting dynamic between the characters.

We often see actors play a character's potency and authority by feigning or bluffing. The body language will be frontal and slightly pushed, with an elevated chin and chest. The bully who leads with his chest is a pushover, not at all dangerous or threatening. The dangerous and truly menacing character is the one who is at ease and fluid in his movement: like the tiger in waiting, he springs instantaneously.

The actor can learn to use his physical presence to diversify his portrayal of power. It is great fun to experiment with the physical aspect of status and dominance in partners. Prior to using language, the body can relate a complex and fascinating story of shifting power and powerlessness. To play one's potency in a confrontation, the body must be fully engaged. To deflate the body by dropping into the hips or collapsing into a contracted 'cool' stance only conveys an attitude, not genuine power.

I delighted in working with a cast of *West Side Story* when, in the early phase of rehearsal, we improvised and played with the tension and hostility between the Jets and the Sharks. Here is an example of how a group of twenty actors explored status through the body.

In a large rehearsal hall, we divided the actors into two groups. The actors were asked to move into the rehearsal space, choosing a high or low status for their character, and to meet another character in the space. By encountering each other in the playing space, they would discover who and what sort of energy confronted them. They were asked to improvise for a brief exchange and then separate, to cross back through the space. A little story was told with every encounter.

Everyone had a turn, while the group watching observed how evident it was when an actor was bluffing his power by overdoing it and pushing in the body. Those actors who chose a lower status tended to collapse and overplay impotence by contracting the body.

I encouraged the actors to think of the volume of the body, to find their backs and also to use the intention of an upward direction as they moved into interaction with the other. As they went through the exercise again, making a new choice and meeting a new character, it was helpful to coach them to continue to breathe, especially as they met. Breath was vital to maintain or gain power.

Breaking the groups into the Jets and the Sharks gave the actors a specific motivation from the play to imagine. The dynamic of a one-on-one confrontation changed immediately when a third player was brought into the playing space. A character of a low status could be immediately elevated by the entrance of an allied energy shifting the power. It is effective to have the actors express themselves solely through the body, without words, so that when the need for language develops they are distinctly connected to what they say physically. Corporeal communication may be all that is needed to portray the story between characters.

I once went to visit my friend Sandra Niman, an Alexander teacher and storyteller, who lives on a ranch on the sea coast of northern Californian with her husband Bill, a big dog, many head of steer and a beautiful green parrot named Juanita. I was telling Sandy about my work with young actors on a dramatic television series about high school. It was my job to coach and choreograph these relatively untrained young television actors in scenes of conflict and teenage antagonism. Sandy was curious to learn how I had used the Alexander Technique to instruct the actors in a confrontational situation. I demonstrated in her kitchen the difference in my movement when I first approached her aggressively by leading with my chest and sticking out my chin in a tough-girl attitude. Then I showed her my example of how I came up and out of my hips while thinking of my whole body and voluminous back as I approached her. With the second example, as I moved towards Sandy, suddenly Juanita flew at me from a ceiling rafter and bit me hard on the ear. Ouch! She drew blood. I had to laugh through my pain to say 'See, it works!'

8. Tableau Exercise – Learning to Survive a 'Freeze'

Most actors at some point in their careers have been asked to create the dreaded 'tableau'. A director will request the actors to hold a pose or freeze an action or gesture for an extended period of time. The director wants to create a stage picture. If the actors are frozen in action, it heightens the theatricality of the stage image. The suffering actor will probably experience murderous thoughts about that director while sustaining a frozen pose for three to ten minutes.

I have seen numerous productions that open with a tableau. The director might establish a picture that depicts a specific era in full period costume. Or characters in grotesque, distorted images of cruelty might serve the director's conception of the world of the play. Every director who demands a tableau of his cast ought to go through the experience of sustaining a shape without moving for at least five minutes, to learn how taxing and physically challenging not moving can be: out on the stage, the frozen actor's muscles will be aching and burning to release.

While maintaining a tableau, the actor will struggle to find breath inconspicuously, so as not to expose their being alive. Albeit extremely subtle, there is always some breath and movement in the body. The audience may not be able to observe movement, but the life force will be there. The actor must be very active mentally when restraining movement in the body in order to survive the demands of sustaining a pose.

No matter how restricted or bizarre the shape an actor creates with his body, there is no reason for him to tighten his neck at the top of his spine. The actor should be able to release his head and neck at the occipital joint, which will create a minute space of freedom at the top of the spine. Understanding how the head organizes itself forward and upwards, away from the body, will enhance the actor's balance. If the actor can apply the Alexander Technique and use his thinking to direct the body to expand and open in an upward direction, he will release the increasing downward pressure and constriction in the body brought on by maintaining the freeze.

The Tableau Exercise

This tableau exercise may be experienced in a group class or individually.

* Have the actors move into creating a contracted or twisted shape.
* Find a position and freeze for three minutes.
* The body will begin to react to the restriction and the actor will get some kinesthetic feedback from areas in the body experiencing some tension or compression
* The feedback may be a sense of panic in the breath, an aching sensation in a muscle, a tremor in a limb, a dizzy light-headedness, drying mouth, or a big pain in the neck.
* As time passes, the areas of discomfort will intensify. Perhaps a burning sensation may develop.
* Take your attention to the occipital joint at the top of the spine, located behind the uvula. Think of freeing your neck there, making a tad more space to allow your head to move ever so slightly.
* Observe the connection between the top and the bottom of the spine. Become aware of the sacrum and the hip joints by directing the pelvis upwards. Have you felt a release of a downward pressure?
* Allow your eyes to look out and move slightly so that you are not staring and fixing your eyeballs. Think of softening your vision.
* Breathe gently through the nose. Does your breath travel into your back? Allow the ribs to expand and contract. This movement of your breathing is very subtle and not noticeable to an audience.
* Soften the front of your ankles and notice the distribution of your weight over the entire foot. Release your toes.
* Think of creating more open space in all your joints. Are your fingers and wrists tightening? Let the joints soften or ease up.

- Consider the full circumference of your limbs and torso. If fatigue is starting to manifest tension in the tops of your arms, think of the support coming up from under and around the three-dimensional limb.
- See how activating your thinking has an immediate kinesthetic response. This conscious constructive thinking will keep you alert and active in the non-active body and help you to sustain your position.
- Check in and release your neck and continue to breathe. You will survive this agony and avoid atrophy if you stay with yourself.
- Hold this for at least three minutes. Time will take on another sense of proportion and pass either very quickly or painfully slowly.
- Release your entire body and shake off the held shape. You will most likely want to jump about a bit.
- Ask yourself if you made a physical choice that you could support and sustain without too much discomfort. Was your shape over-extended and too difficult to maintain. Could you establish a similar shape without overextending?
- See how this exercise works over the course of five minutes. Repeat your configuration and make any modifications necessary, or throw out your last choice and make a new and simpler shape.
- When asked to create a tableau, the old adage 'less is more' is relevant. Never be too zealous and create a shape that is extraordinary but too physically taxing, especially in those early tableau rehearsals, as you may live to regret the choice further down the line of a long run. Do a bit less and you will maintain and manage the five-minute freeze more easily.

The Table Work and the Alexander Technique

With many Alexander Technique teachers, the table work is a significant component of the Alexander Technique. The teachers use the table in order to open the joints and lengthen and widen the musculature of the student without the demands of weight-bearing and support of an upright stance. The table work provides an opportunity for the actor to observe his body in a relaxed and supported manner. The Alexander Technique teacher can ascertain the organizational habits of the student's muscular-skeletal system in this relatively neutral lying-down position. In other words, the teacher can observe holding patterns and predominant tension areas in the body.

F. M. Alexander felt that the lying-down work was a simple way to focus the student's physical awareness and to practise inhibition. As the teacher moves the limbs of the body, the student is able to inhibit the first response they have to the teacher's touch. Then the student can give the mental direction to free the neck and release any response to tighten.

Observation of the student is essential before the teacher begins to put their hands on the body. The hands of the Alexander teacher are trained; they are sensing tools and the teacher's means of discovering kinesthetically and intellectually what is happening in the student's body. The teacher's hands are also the means for communicating ëdirection', which is the given stimulus for the body to move in a new and non-habitual way. The quality of the hands on contact in the Alexander work should be delicate, clear and subtle. The Alexander experience is different from a massage or a therapeutic manipulative technique. With the Alexander work, the student has a responsibility to participate by remaining mentally alert in order to become aware, to inhibit a habitual response and to redirect his body.

The object of the table work is to heighten awareness of any holding or constriction in the joints and muscles. With the gentle guidance of the Alexander teacher's hands, the student will be encouraged to free the neck and lengthen and widen the back muscles as well as to release extraneous contractions of the joints in the limbs. The process of learning to let go is a bit scary. The student must embrace a willingness to explore the unknown in a kinesthetic realm which is full of unfamiliar sensation and sensory feedback. The table provides a steady support for the body in this new experience. The table used would be similar to a basic massage table or a flat-top table about six feet long and at an appropriate height for the teacher to access the student in a prone position. One actor observed:

> When I think of the Alexander table work, it is like that eastern idea of 'mindfulness', that it is not passive, it is actually being aware, noticing and quietly observing what is going on with you in little minute ways, whether that is in your thoughts or in your body. It is all about seeing what is going on and therefore giving you more energy to go forward. Rather than thinking of how tense and confused you are in your body, it allows you take a moment just to do nothing but pay attention to what is going on in your body and what that triggers.

Here are two examples of how the Alexander teacher might work with an actor on the table. I had worked with the actors in these example lessons before and so I was familiar with their bodies. We worked together to identify and overcome some of the problem areas in their bodies. The work is subtle and requires the student to stay alert and open to the hands-on experience with the teacher.

Lesson One

When inviting the actor to lie down on his back, face up on the table, I ask him to remember that the skeleton has many joints and to think of moving the skeleton in order to reduce his motivation and emphasize movement predominantly by the muscles. Once he is lying on his back, I will place a few books under his head to support the weight of the head/skull in a forward relationship to the top of the spine. I encourage him to allow the table to support his whole body. I request that he observes the points of contact his body is making with the table. Does he notice the differences he might have on either side of his torso? Are the bones and muscles of his legs organized uniformly or is there a difference between one leg and the other? This particular actor has long legs. He thinks he has a short-waisted torso. I suggest that he should consider the length he has in the body, envision his body as one long unit and keep the head/neck and back unified. I ask him to inhibit the holding in his leg and to release into the support of my hands as a means to open and free up the leg from the hip joint. Then, together, we direct each leg to lengthen away from the torso while bending the knee into the semi-supine position. With the knees bent and the feet on the table, he notices that his lower back has opened slightly, increasing his contact with the table.

We focus our attention on engaging the muscles in his lower body to support his upper body through extending each of his arms up over his head. When he is directed to move his arms, I ask him to notice his first response to my direction. He notices that he initiates the movement from his shoulder. I ask him to inhibit his initial or habitual response when directed to move his arm, and instead to think of initiating the arm's movement from his fingers, keeping the joints active as he outstretches the arm. Having engaged his thinking to respond to this simple movement with a new thought and direction, it allows his shoulders and upper arms to follow freely and sequentially without constriction in the joints and contraction in the muscles. He discovers how the support and the origin of his arms comes from his back, allowing his muscles to lengthen and widen across his chest and his back. When preparing to get up from the table, he has to inhibit his response to tighten and push off the table. His attention needs to stay with the direction of freeing his neck as he rolls on to his side and then he has to lead with his head, to allow his body to follow as he rolls up into a sitting position.

When he gets up off the table, I observe a more open and spacious upper back. While walking around, he experiences increased freedom to move his upper arms and chest. He makes the connection to have his lower body widen and give support to his upper back. This gives him a unified experience of the whole body moving.

Lesson Two

I have worked with this actress many times and I am aware that her body is very sensitive. Working in a lying-down position, I ask her to think of engaging her energy up from and through the arches in her feet in order to inhibit her tendency to turn in at her knees and misalign her legs. It is odd for her to think up and to include her inner thighs as a way to change the use of her leg. We work on softening the tendons at the front of her ankles to allow more movement and flexion across the foot in order to distribute her weight better when she is standing upright.

She contracts her upper arms, compressing her shoulders and closing off her armpits. The pressure of her arms against her ribs causes an undue tension and restriction throughout her shoulder girdle. I put my hands under her shoulder, as a means to contact the point of the insertion of her *latissimus dorsi* muscle (see the charts in the Anatomy Lesson section) in the underside of her arms. My hands encourage her awareness to allow some release and freedom in the arms and shoulders. Her tendency is to allow her arms to become a dead weight, which pulls down her whole body. We work at inhibiting the response of tightening in her upper arms, thus allowing the arms to release without collapsing her sternum and frontal support.

She needs to pay attention to her breathing as we work, so as not to hold her breath in response to the stimulus of my hands. We are successful in connecting her lower body with the upward and outward breadth and width of her shoulders. She allows a good deal of movement and release through her sacrum in her lower back. While my hands are under the sacrum and pelvic area, I propose the simple thought of directing the pelvis upwards towards the ceiling, which allows the sacrum to release and the muscles to lengthen towards her head. This happens without manipulating the pelvis to go in that direction, but by simply creating enough space and room for the body to release of its own volition.

I enjoy working with this actress because she responds to the lightest touch and direction of my hands. She has a highly tuned sensitivity to the life in her body. The thinking process of giving Alexander's direction and the concept of 'non-doing' is highly effective for her body.

Every actor is different. The Alexander teacher needs to adapt and respond to a varied range of kinesthetic sensibility and awareness of the body with each student in the table work. The gentleness and opening aspect of the table work is ideal for the actor under the pressure and stress of opening a play or shooting a film. Quiet work can be very calming and collects the actor's energy and state of mind.

PART 3

Alexander Technique and Voice Work

1. Alexander's Discovery

F. M. Alexander made his discovery when searching for some answers to why and how he was losing his voice. Through an actor's diligence, discipline and keen powers of observation, he made a scientific discovery about the workings of the mind and body. I have already described Alexander's experience of vocal problems and how that led him to study the cause of his vocal tension and subsequently evolve the Alexander Technique in the introductory section on 'F. M. Alexander's Story'. It is an actor's nightmare to lose his voice or to be unable to speak his lines. Anyone who has experienced vocal troubles will tell you a painful tale of fear and anxiety. One actress who has battled with vocal issues says:

> I have had vocal nodules on my vocal cords three times in my life and I have never had them surgically removed, but I came close to it. I was frightened that I would forfeit my burgeoning career. Not unlike Alexander's voice problem and losing his voice, I think my problems and bad habit of putting pressure on my vocal cords developed through my youthful, zealous energy of pushing to produce my voice. I think with my knowledge of the Alexander Technique and with the voice work, I am more sensitive to when I overdo it or when I go into a misuse of my voice. I am more aware of when I am pushing. Now I can start to redirect myself instead of having it drive out of my control and so far those nodes have not returned and I hope they never will! To me, the voice work and the Alexander work are inseparable. They can each help me through certain specific problems separately, but together they are a perfect

team. I can't do one without the other because breath and thought are who you are.

F. M. Alexander's recovery of his voice enabled him to make many discoveries that people have been learning from long after his death. His 'actor spirit' would be well satisfied to know that his voice work was still reaching an audience night after night in the theatre.

2. Voice Work and the Alexander Technique

In the Alexander Technique, we focus a great deal of attention on the relationship of the head, neck and back. We consider that the primary control is a major component in the human being's coordination. What makes the human being unique and arguably superior to other animals is our ability to use rational thought and mental power to direct our coordination. We can engage our thinking to redirect how we use our bodies.

The vocal mechanism is housed in the throat where the head and the neck conjoin. Heightening an awareness in this area of the body is significant for comprehending the voice. Sound is created by breath resonating in the body. The skeleton and bony structure of the body provides the sounding board for the breath to resonate off. The freer we are in the skeleton and the muscles, the more space and capacity we have for creating sound. Therefore it makes a great deal of sense to educate the performer about the body and its movement potential.

Technically, we know that if the body is locked, it will restrict the breath. Breath is essential for voice production. For example, we know that if you lock your knees, it is difficult to achieve a full support of the voice. The lower back and pelvis are locked into a fixed position when the legs are set because the femur of the leg comes into the hip socket and restricts the movement of the entire pelvis. One always wants to have the potential to move at the hip joint. When we are standing or sitting still, the option to move from the hips should be available. Otherwise, the body will settle down on to the joints, creating downward pressure in the body and restricting freedom of movement in the joints. When we release the downward pressure and allow the body to move forward and upward, the body will move with greater ease and the subtle movement of breathing will also improve.

When we first observe our breath, we observe the habitual rhythm and movement of breathing, or perhaps the absence of movement and a lack of breath. Engaging our thought to remember to breathe is a physical activity. One actor describes the process thus:

> When I give myself Alexander direction, there are changes that help me as an actor. When I am lengthened, I'm better balanced and literally more open, I feel larger and open in all my cavities. When I direct myself up and lengthen, I also experience widening. You can feel your chest unlock and your back free up when you have had a good Alexander lesson. It allows you to breathe more easily so you are not fighting through tension to breathe. You often see actors muscling their breath down or forgetting to breathe. When you open up and have a greater sense of awareness, you don't have to think of the breathing so much. You are just doing it and it seems to go down further, down below the belt, into the groin. When I am sunken in the chest, that is where my breath stops, but if I lengthen I can feel the breath fill my lungs. Consequently the voice coming back out doesn't have obstacles in the way. When I breathe easily, I can get to the emotional places I need to go in order to effectively communicate what it is I'm acting in the moment. With the heightened language of a classical text, it is the readiness of an emotional state that is useful. With the character Claudio in *Measure for Measure*, my breathing got better after applying the Alexander directions. By taking my time and not forgetting to breathe, the emotions came, as opposed to trying to put the emotions on; they were coming out on the breath. Alexander helps me to get out of my way.

The Alexander teacher can be very helpful to the actor with regard to the voice. Personally, I am inspired and excited by the collaborative process of joining forces with the expertise of the voice teacher. Actors and singers must consider how the instrument or vessel of the voice is housed in the body. It is meaningful for the actor to make the connection between the freeing of the body and the freedom of the breath and voice.

Together, the two disciplines of voice work and the Alexander Technique can inform the actor's awareness and command of his vocal energy and production. A collaborative dialogue between the voice teacher and the Alexander teacher can be very productive and insightful. It is helpful to learn from one another when coaching individual actors. We can solve problems more effectively when insights are shared.

A voice teacher colleague expresses from her point of view how the Alexander work complements voice work:

Today I saw a young actress who arrived at voice class on the verge of tears because she thinks she has vocal nodules. As she lay down and I talked her through her breath, I observed her shoulders were up around her ears. I knew this was not a voice problem, but it was a physical problem which was getting in the way of her voice. This is what I find so complementary in the work, that often I see someone and I think they need to go off and do six months of Alexander and then come back and we will work on their voice, because to me the voice comes out of the body. The Alexander Technique does not mean having the perfect body, it is about how you are using it and finding the freedom in it.

In terms of working in the classical theatre, the Alexander work is an integral part of the process. Vocally, the actor must fill the space and have a sense of the arc in the text and thought. If the actor can think up and out physically, then the voice will naturally go there. It is not about trying to get your voice out there or projecting the voice. I hate that word 'projection'. To me, the voice is about thought, so that if the actor is already thinking in that physical realm, the voice just goes there because the voice wants to go there. To me, the voice is three-dimensional and that's where it marries with the body. I find it a natural connection.

I use the Alexander language of 'inhibition' when I am working with an actor who wants to pump their breath. F. M. Alexander used the word to 'inhibit' this desire to push the breath. I find in the breath work when the student is able to stop the pushing they may experience all sorts of feelings; tremendous anxiety, frustration, panic, often people feel they are suffocating because they can't muscle the breathe in a way they are used to doing. I use the principle of inhibition in my teaching to encourage the actor to stay with himself, to keep talking to himself, to tell himself that he is not going to suffocate and to stay with the breath in order to come on to the voice without pushing or overdoing it. It is through this conscious process that the voice will change and become freer.

3. Musical Theatre

Most singers come to the musical theatre with a great deal of vocal training. The singer/dancer/actor is often the most energetic and physically fit of all thespians. They have trained to move and sing at the same time which is very demanding for the body. Musical-theatre folk are a special breed who seem to me to have the most fun in the theatrical experience.

The Alexander Technique is often the first technique the singer/dancer encounters that addresses both voice and body simultaneously. They are usually very responsive to the ideas of balance and organization of the body. The musical performer is so often asked to 'sell it', or to exaggerate and produce a vigorous musical-comedy energy. The Alexander Technique can help them to counteract this overdrive by learning to perform with ease and relaxation, avoiding any pushing and overdoing it.

I was amused to observe the dancer/ singers in the early days of rehearsal for the musical *Gypsy*. Several of the performers had worked with the choreographer before and were familiar with his creative process and propensity to change his mind on the trot. The 'first-timers' would rehearse the dance numbers full out, keen and effervescent; the 'old-timers' knew to pace their energy by going through the number marking time. It was amusing to pick out the new kids on the block. The rehearsal process is the time to learn, not the time to go for broke; as the character Mama Rose would have it, 'Sing out Louise!' The triple-thread performer must protect the voice and body from overworking since the director will often ask for full-throttle energy before it is time.

Janine Pearson, the head of the voice department, approached me during the rehearsal of *The Music Man*. The star of the show was experiencing vocal strain. We discussed his vocal problem and she told me of his fear of losing his voice. Janine is knowledgeable about Alexander work. She observed him pushing his head forwards and contracting in his neck, especially in the patter song 'Trouble in River City', which was creating a great deal of tension in his chest and neck. This performer had long, long, elegant legs; he was loose as a goose, tap dancing being his forte. We agreed that he needed to bring his focus and awareness up into his upper body, specifically to the relationship of his head to his neck and back.

Our 'music man' identified that he had been pushing. He was open to having a joint class with the Alexander teacher, the voice teacher and the company pianist to experiment together. We learned that he had strained his back playing the lead dance role during a long run of the musical *Crazy for You*. As dancers tend to mend on the job, he was probably still healing and repairing. As the show was being staged on a thrust stage, attention needed to be paid to playing the three-dimensional aspect of the venue. The actor needs to see up and out in order to open his contact with an encircling audience. With the thrust stage, the actor will have his back to a portion of the audience at all times. He will naturally feel exposed in a similar way to being 'in the round' and he will sense the need to communicate more fully or three-dimensionally. Like most musical-theatre actors, the 'music man' was more familiar with the proscenium-arch theatre. In the last section of this book, I discuss the issue of playing the space in a variety of theatrical venues.

We suggested that the 'music man' inhibit his need to push his face forwards to meet the on-stage audience, the townsfolk of River City. He had the habit of pushing his face forward to communicate and articulate, but we encouraged him simply to trust his 6'2" statuesque height to draw all the audience into his character. We worked on the music man's big number, the salesman's pitch, 'Trouble in River City'. With the joint expertise of the voice coach and the Alexander teacher's 'hands-on' input, we helped him make the connection between the articulation of language in a patter song with staying up and out in the body. When he was able to stop the habitual contraction of his head and sustained seeing up and out, the language became clearer and easier.

As an Alexander teacher, I was able to place my hands on his head and neck while the voice teacher coached him vocally. The idea was to have him endow the townsfolk with 'trouble' while he observed them from his place of worldly know-how, using his wonderfully long limbs as a means of sending energy away from himself, out to his fellow actors and the audience. As the character, Harold Hill, he had a habit of touching his mouth, face and head which tended to return his energy back into himself, causing him to contract his energy rather than expand it. When he used his full stature and remained centred, he was able to articulate the language and generate focus to direct the attention of his audience with less effort and tension.

Through this collaborative process, the actor was able to apply and integrate information *tout de suite*. Happily, the problem was detected early enough in rehearsal and he changed his pattern. He was able to perform the entire run of the show without ever losing his voice.

One season, I became familiar with the work and the body of a leading actress/singer/dancer in a musical. I would describe her as a beautiful soprano, highly feminine and easily cast as Guinevere, the romantic lead in *Camelot*. The next season, she faced a totally different casting challenge, playing Aldonza in *Man of La Mancha*. Aldonza is a prostitute, who describes herself as 'a kitchen slut reeking of sweat, a strumpet men use and forget'. This is a far cry from the romantic characters of *Camelot*. Perhaps the greatest physical challenge for her in *Camelot* had been her twelve rapid-fire costume changes. In *Man of La Mancha*, she had only one costume. However, she had a huge dance number that closed with a nasty gang-rape scene.

Aldonza's songs require a belt voice with a good deal of raunchy physicality in the staging. I observed our Aldonza working too hard and struggling in the initial stage of developing the crude and low-born character. In search of the character's vulgarity, she chose to contract her head and neck, sticking her chin out to curse the men taunting her. This choice created an appropriate lewd shape in her upper body, but it was creating vocal stress. I observed the tension and strain in her neck and I knew she needed to become aware of the head contracting and to engage more from her lower body to get the support vocally. She was very open to input, so we arranged a rehearsal with the piano. We thought we might solve the problem with the help of some 'hands-on' Alexander Technique applied directly to the singer in character. When she observed her response to playing Aldonza involved contracting her head and neck, she was able to let it go. Being a dancer and a quick study, she just took on the new information and immediately reorganized her body in the process of performing the song. By freeing up her neck and her awareness of engaging her lower body for support, the singing became easier. She could create the belt sound without the pressure on her vocal mechanism. I suggested she think of Aldonza's arias as making an 'ovarian' argument.

It was exciting to hear her voice and see her body adapt so quickly. She was off and strutting her strumpet with an open stride, released knees and ankles and playing from her lower centre. We joked that finding her lower centre was 'yoni power'! We had a lot of fun getting 'up', not 'down and dirty', in that rehearsal.

4. Opera Singing and the Alexander Technique

The opera singer is another breed entirely. Opera singers are most concerned with the sound they are making, no matter what they have to do with themselves to create a beautiful sound. They are very aware that their singing instrument is housed inside the body. Singers will make a great fuss about keeping their necks warm with scarves and will avoid consumption of dairy products and sip herbal tea concoctions to aid and protect the voice. However, it is curious how little singers tend to know about the anatomy and organization of the body. They are generally far less concerned about physical fitness than the average actor. Elevating breathing aerobically on a Stairmaster or the treadmill is not the daily routine of opera singers; singing tends to be their physical activity.

When watching a singer in a recital, the audience can relax when the performance seems effortless and the performer is at ease with the job. It is distracting to observe an artist struggle with tension and strain throughout the performance. We have all seen the lovely soprano smiling and performing happily, until we notice that all her tension has manifested in one hand and it is beating out the time like a lobster clawing away at her velvet gown. Once you notice that tense hand, you can't take your eyes off it and you begin to worry about the poor gal and whether she will survive her ordeal. When the aria is over, you sigh with relief. The singer would be horrified to learn that members of her audience were so conscious of her habit of physical tension that they were removed from the music.

If a performer can identify and then release the 'overdoing' aspect in their work, they will be freer to express themselves artistically. This is where applying the Alexander principle of ease and non-doing can be very fruitful.

A voice teacher colleague relates her experience to the Alexander Technique process:

First of all, I trained as a classical singer, and then as an actor, so I have studied singing and then the speaking voice work. As a young person in school, I felt the true joy of singing and I lost that in train-ing. In retrospect, I see that I lost the joy through acquired physical tension. I am by nature an 'endgainer' so the acquisition of tension became a part of the process to achieve my goals. That tension sent me on a journey about voice. I wondered how did the singing voice and the speaking voice fit together? When I went to school in England to become a voice teacher, I started some Alexander Technique work. My Alexander teacher did all his classes on the table. He would get me on the table and we would begin working and he would be talking to me and I realized that I could not talk back, I literally could not physicalize speaking. During the lesson, I would lose my voice. The experience of the Alexander work and the physical changes meant I could not produce my voice in the way I had learned to do it. The most profound thing in the Alexander Technique for me, as a voice person, was realizing that I had to lose my voice in order to find it again. That work positively changed my life; everything that I thought and struggled with in singing and voice work, changed.

5. The Whispered 'Ah' Exercise

As F. M. Alexander went through the personal struggle and painful experience of vocal troubles, he was always observant of how he used his voice. He developed his Alexander Technique with many students, not just actors with vocal problems and voice-related interests. He developed a useful procedure or exercise which he called the 'whispered "ah"'.

Teaching the 'whispered "ah"' was a way of applying Alexander's principles of inhibition and direction to the breath and the release of sound without creating tension and pressure on the vocal mechanism. It helps to enhance freedom in the jaw and the tongue. He wanted the student to have the experience of making a sound without the habitual pattern or strain of pushing for vocal production. The flow of air and a subtle 'ah' sound should be very gentle and non-restrictive.

The exercise can be done sitting or standing. Here is my version of the sequence of instructions Alexander taught.

● See out, with your eyes open and alert.
● Free your neck by thinking of the freedom at the occipital joint, located at the top of the spine, directly behind the uvula.
● Allow your tongue to relax and rest on the floor of your mouth.
● Place the tip of your tongue at ease behind your bottom front teeth.
● Check in with the jaw bone adjacent to the earlobe to see that you are not clenching or holding the jaw shut. Your back molar teeth should not be touching.
● Are you breathing?
● Think of something naughty or mischievous, as if you were keeping a secret. If the secret is naughty enough you will sense a smile in the musculature of the face and a twinkle in your eye.
● Maintain the smile as you free the jaw to open the mouth. The tip of the tongue continues to contact the lower teeth.
● Release a very gentle, soft 'ah' sound.
● Sustain the gentle 'ah' sound until you come to the end of your breath. Avoid tightening and pushing at the end of your breath.
● Simply allow your lips to close gently.
● When you close your lips, do you sense how freely and easily the

breath comes in through your nose and into your body?
* Relax. Don't rush this process. Breathe and repeat these steps.
* Observe how the soft palate (the soft cushion-like area at the roof of your mouth where we see your uvula) opens as the jaw releases to create a more open space at the back of your throat.
* Keep that mischievous thought ongoing, to maintain that important gentle smile.
* Maintain freedom in the neck muscles.
* Allow the breath to release at its own pace and rhythm.
* Do not push the sound out.
* With each repetition, one should sense a growing freedom and ease in the jaw.
* Perhaps you will feel an extension of the breath and an increased depth to the inhalation.
* Are the ribs swinging freely?
* Try this about six to eight times. One can experiment while driving in the car on the way to work or include it in a voice warm-up.

PART 4
The Alexander Technique and Acting Challenges

Relevance of the Alexander Technique to Acting

1. The Actor and Fitness

Not all actors are fit, although it would seem an obvious career enhancement to be fit. The current fitness culture has come to the theatre. Hearing the young members of the acting company talking about the previous evening spent at the gym, one older, seasoned actor joked, 'Hey, what's wrong with you? Are you sure you are actors? Don't you get drunk, smoke a million cigarettes, a few joints and have wild sex? That is what we did when I was your age!' In this rapidly changing world, the consciousness of the actor has changed with the times. These days, most actors, young and old, are committed to fitness.

A career in acting is always physically demanding. The individual actor knows how he must prepare and maintain his own body to meet the rigours of the job. Alexander work is not an exercise; it addresses how we exercise. The Alexander Technique and its various principles can be applied to all movement work. We can learn to rethink and redirect our approach to exercising. Actors must notice the quality of movement and learn a method to perform any exercise with ease and relaxation.

An astute mind and body is imperative for the acting craft. The Alexander Technique is an adaptable tool which, when used properly, will support the actor throughout the exploration of a theatrical undertaking.

All emotional experiences have a physical component. The body is along for the ride when we are shocked, saddened or elated. The body gives the experience expression. The connection of the mind and body is crucial for the actor. Often the actor has to relive and retell a story for eight shows a week. Gaining knowledge and sensitivity of the body frees the actor to test and explore his physical and emotional range.

As we proceed, we see how the Alexander work is directly and practically relevant to acting. We shall examine the application of the Alexander work in a variety of theatrical exercises and issues. Characterization, mask work, nudity, animal study, costumes, wigs, kissing, physical comedy, injuries and ageing are some of the theatrical dilemmas that face the actor. Actors will discuss their experiences of using the Alexander Technique to address problems encountered in rehearsal.

2. Character Work and the Alexander Technique

Often actors will come to the Alexander class with concerns and questions about the effect a character is having on the body. Actors constantly struggle with issues of tension and restriction in the freedom of their movement. Let's face it, there is an enormous amount of tension in drama.

First, I will ask an actor to find and perform the character in order to observe closely how the body is organized. I need to learn how the actor has chosen to shape his character physically. I want to learn where the downward pressure and tensions are in his body, to discern whether we can relieve excessive strain and to analyse how best to support the body given the choice the actor is making.

The Alexander teacher's input must be very sensitive to the actor so as not to interfere or impose too much on the actor's creative process with an Alexander agenda of 'good use'. Here, I may apply the hands-on aspect of the Alexander Technique to investigate what the actor's body is doing. A teacher may suggest a subtle movement with their hands to release the head and neck. The neck often creates extraneous tension and will tighten in response to an imposed change in the actor's body. An actor can always free the neck at the occipital joint, no matter how contracted the shape he may want his body to portray. The head-and-neck relationship can always maintain freedom, allowing the body and spine to create any shape from below the occipital joint.

The Alexander concept of the 'primary control' can be very useful for the actor to avoid strain and injury. The Alexander teacher may stimulate the joints and muscles to release excessive holding and appeal to another part of the body to furnish support in an area that demands some strain and tension.

The Alexander Technique teacher can also help the actor with both self-discovery and character discovery. The character has to evolve out of the actor's mind, body and emotions and reside there truthfully, to experience the story of the play moment by moment. The greater the actor's sensitivity and awareness of his body, the wider the range of choices or responses he can make for himself and his characters. The body is the actor's creative instrument, which requires fine tuning, finesse and precision.

One leading actor describes how:

> I was playing two uptight parts, Angelo and Malvolio, and in both those performances something occurred which made me realize that the Alexander Technique was important to my acting and not just something to do to help my back problem. In the final act of Shakespeare's *Measure for Measure*, Angelo is uncovered as the villain that the audience already knows him to be. He must stand there experiencing his tragedy. Of course, he is in this state of extreme tension because all these dreadful revelations about him are being exposed. I discovered that I didn't have to stay in this state of tension, that I could let it all go and then re-experience it in a way that was more interesting for the audience because it wasn't fixed; it was something that I could let go of and then go into a different phase of Angelo's experience. I did not get into one bound state. I found if I released my neck and thought of my head lightening and my back lengthening and widening, I felt that I could become less rigid; thereby able to react to the accumulation of the tension mounting in the scene.

I have worked with a few actors and their understudies on their approach to playing the character of Richard III, the infamous hunchback king. One actor reminded me of the work we did together in preparation for his Richard III:

When faced with the challenge of playing a character like Richard III, first of all you start with a body shape that is going to be believable, not a body shape that is so bizarre that one doesn't look at anything else or hear the story. The audience should be able to take it in with one view; you don't want the body to be the focus where the audience only watches the body and misses the words. The physical choice has to be believable and comfortable, because you have to do it day after day. One must avoid doing permanent damage. You don't want to come away saying, 'I still cannot walk properly because of that Richard III.' Actors can make that mistake, they go too far and they overstress the body for an end that maybe interesting, but it costs them too much. Whatever physicality we came up with for Richard III, it never hurt me, ever. It was a workout, but I never felt that I was in a compromising position that I would have to pay for later down the line. I was able to climb scaffolding, jump off it, move quickly and finish the play with a one-handed sword fight. It is interesting that Shakespeare does not give Richard III any sword-fighting until the very end, which is the actor's only chance to show that character in his element. Richard III is a warrior; your audience has to see that he is a good fighter, despite his physical problems; it's the ace up his sleeve. I must say that my Richard III was done with very little tension. We had talked about strapping in the one arm with a belt or some hook or strap. But we did not use anything. The Alexander Technique helped me find a way to hold the arm for the entire duration of the play and not gather tension; the arm could stay there relaxed and it did not move. I could do front rolls and all kinds of things with the shape of Richard III's body. We created the limp by simply elevating one shoe. The elevated foot made a shift in my hip joints; however, the Alexander work helped me to come up and out of the hips, which allowed me to move freely. For me, the hips are the area where I hold most of my tension, so it is not an area that I wanted to aggravate or strain. Happily, it did not become a problem so long as I stayed relaxed and loose in the hips. Never after a performance did I feel a twinge or any pain. I would credit the ongoing Alexander work with maintaining my flexibility throughout the run of the season. I must have been truly comfortable with the body of Richard

III because at the beginning of the next season, when rehearsing Cassius in *Julius Caesar*, the director pointed out that I was rocking when I was walking. I knew immediately that it was a hang-over from the last year's Richard III. In my opinion, once you find a comfortable body shape, it runs like a well-oiled machine; it's like an engine, it actually supports and moves you from one feeling to the next. You can feel this forward thrust. It is interesting that my body memory seized on to it when my Cassius needed more engine, that I unconsciously went into 'Richard III' mode. '*Et tu*, Ricardo . . .' He'll help you out.

An understanding of how the actor's joints and muscles are involved in the creation of the character's body, be it an extraordinary or a simple shape, will enhance and support the actor's choice. There is a good deal of focus and concentration on the actor knowing how to make the journey into the extension of a character. It is also vital that he understands how to make the return journey home to his neutral body before he leaves the theatre. Who wants to meet for a beer after the show with an actor holding on to remnants of Iago or Claudius in his body?

The Alexander Technique can be a terrific diagnostic tool for the actor to use when he is exploring the boundaries of a character. It helps the actor ensure that he maintains balance and flexibility no matter how fantastic the staging. And the freedom of the body will in turn help the voice to withstand the rigours of a physically demanding show.

One actress whose exciting career in the classical theatre I have watched develop for almost twenty years expresses how she sees the Alexander Technique help her acting process:

Being available is essential to begin a rehearsal and yet self-protection is an issue. With risky exploration, the acting dynamic is based on trust. This is an acting thing, but it does tie in to the Alexander principle of 'letting go'. The acting dynamic requires a willingness to let go; willingness to let go of your past reputation or the status of what you have done before, letting go of your conception of what a character is, or how a scene should be. All these things need to be let go of in order to really do work because they will just hamper you. The body is a good place to focus and to practise the craft of letting go. When you release tension or a habit of holding in a shoulder or the lower back, there is an opening up that allows you to be vulnerable in that place. That's the paradox: in some rehearsals you have to be vulnerable and open to new things while you are trying to survive with some shield of armour. Sometimes when you do an Alexander class and you really go with it and open up your body, it can trigger emotional responses because that holding place has opened up, you are not storing that pain or tension and when the body is released of that tension, other things are triggered and available.

I once helped an actor use Alexander work to rethink a character choice.

In *The Merry Wives of Windsor*, Peter Simple is a comic character and my immediate tendency was to make him a nerd by sinking down and hunching the shoulders, which is fine for a still visual but as far as doing any high physical comedy goes, my choice was a hindrance for my movement. Also, it is harder for the audience to be drawn in to the character when you close yourself off in that hunched-up way. After discussing my character in an Alexander tutorial, I decided to try another option. I lengthened up through my body so that I was almost floating on my toes and this still gave me the nerdish quality but it also allowed me to balance. I was always over the top of my feet, I was able to move very quickly and lightly while still maintaining the character.

One actress describes how the Alexander Technique unveiled chronic tension to which she had become habituated, and how that tension was limiting her acting:

My first contact with the Alexander work came at the start of my professional career. Not having had much body work, I was just beginning to recognize what tension was. I had a lot of tension evident in my acting work, yet I could not identify it very well. I failed to realize that my shoulders were up to my ears or that my neck stuck out in order to emphasize a point. When playing Imogen in *Cymbeline*, I realized I had this monumental emotional task. It was my first leading role and a high-pressure rehearsal situation. During rehearsal, there were places I was unable to get to because I was too tight, tense and nervous. So there I was, getting Alexander training on a very tense body. What does 'freeing the neck' really mean when you can't remember what it was ever like to have a free head and neck? But gradually, with the ongoing Alexander lessons, little by little, I began to feel my strength as a performer. I realized that my head was actually staying on top of the body and it wasn't being thrust forward. It was exciting to realize that a strong back has loose shoulders. I did improve as the Alexander concepts became clearer for me during the run of *Cymbeline*. It helped me become more comfortable in the role and I had more access to the emotion. Imogen was an interesting role to play because she is in so much pain. The play starts out at such a high emotional level, with Imogen experiencing the worst pain in her life. For me, learning to allow the body to register all that pain and not be completely locked with tension was my challenge. I really associate that role with the beginning of understanding that I had all this tension and if I could lose it I would have a much easier and happy time in my acting. My body certainly improved as we went along and I became more aware of the Alexander work in my life.

3. Playing Another Gender – from the 'Trouser Role' to the Drag Act

Playing the opposite sex is primarily a movement problem. Often in the Shakespeare repertoire we call it the 'trouser' or 'pant' role, where the female disguises herself as a male, as with Viola in *Twelfth Night*, Rosalind in *As You Like It* and Imogen in *Cymbeline*. Ironically, in Shakespeare's time the female roles were played by young boys, so you would have had a boy playing a girl playing a boy. Now, that is a gender bender!

For the most part, an actress who is playing a role where she must pretend she is male tends to focus her attention by sitting in the pelvis and then walking about leading from the hips. This choice of leading with imagined male genitalia pulls her body down, shortens her stature and restricts her range of movement and flexibility in the lower body. As it is very likely that while portraying a man she will have some stage combat or demanding staging, she will need her flexibility. In working with many actress on the male movement issues, I have discovered that with closer observation of generic male movement, the male has a slightly higher centre of gravity. Males tend to carry most tension in the legs from pushing down through the leg to stay up off the hips. There is much less swing in the hips compared to the female. The female will most likely experience more tension in the inner thighs and a restriction of movement in the pelvic floor. These changes can be experimented with, under the guidance of the Alexander teacher, in order to play the other sex with as much freedom as possible.

An actress recalls her experience of Rosalind and Viola:

I remember wondering what the difference was going to be before I took on Viola. Rosalind was a gift, she just sat right on me, a case of the right moment at the right time, but Viola was not as easy a fit for me. I don't know why. The thing to do was to find out what was different about Viola; she was not at all like Rosalind. I had to find out what kind of a boy was she. For the most part, the clues and answers are in the text. For Viola, it is much more of a social structure that she moves into and Rosalind moves from a social structure into the open and unstructured freedom of the forest. Rosalind can be free physically and mentally as a boy in a man's world, whereas for Viola it is the complete opposite; she becomes totally restricted as a boy in a man's world. And therein lie the clues to how the body must move and how the actress might feel in those diverse worlds. The body will be expressive of the character's experience in the play.

The journey of exploring another gender is indeed a physical trip. A man in drag is a common theatrical device. Observing and admiring the opposite sex can be useful when playing the opposite sex. Think of the comedic gender turns of the *Monty Python* troupe and the *Kids in the Hall*. When conceiving a female character, men need to soften and release the musculature. Men believe in a taut, firm sensation in the muscles. When they preen, they pump up the musculature. The female body has a softer and more supple musculature. Women allow more flexion and freedom in the joints when they move. There is much more action in the hip joints. The male actor must be cautious not to flounce and over-produce the movement in the hips and shoulders. In their earnest imagining of breasts, they tend to hyper-extend the chest and lean back, which contracts and inhibits freedom in the lower back.

Men will be challenged by the female costume and accoutrements. One season, in a production of *Troilus and Cressida*, the director's concept was to have the Greek army in drag. I was presented with the coaching problem of twenty young actors in wigs and high heels parading on a raked stage in drag. *Ay Carumba!* Generally, most of the men were overstriding in the high heels, which, compounded by the raked stage, made it murderous on the lower back. When an actor shortened his stride, he could balance forward and upwards over the shoe. This also helped the actor to come up off the hip joints, which enhanced the feminine aspect of moving.

One actor recalls his struggle:

It is quite an education to play the other sex, because one takes for granted the amount of power you have in society or in a rehearsal situation, as a man. It is interesting how vulnerable-making it is to truly let the masculinity go. Some actors, when playing a woman, are constantly letting the audience know that they are a man playing a woman, as if winking at them. They never really let it go and go for it. I obviously can't be a woman, but I want to explore the feminine side of myself and give over to it. It takes a certain amount of confidence in yourself to not constantly let them know with some little clue that you are a guy. Not to be apologizing or feeling the need to say this is dumb, sending out those vibes, because you are afraid. The most rewarding part of playing a woman was really going for it. I remember calling an actress friend and complaining that I was having a difficult time in rehearsal for Caryl Churchill's *Cloud Nine*. The play has cross-gender casting and I played a Victorian woman in the second act. She asked 'How's your frock?' I responded 'It's wonderful, I love it.' She said, 'Well, good. In the next rehearsal, when everything goes to rat shit, just twirl, twirl, twirl.'

4. Imitation – Mirroring

In Part 2, we explored how mirroring or twinning exercises are helpful in developing young actors' skills of observation, imitation, rhythm and physical organization of the 'other'. One of the oldest theatrical tricks in the book is the convention of 'twinning', as in Shakespeare's *Comedy of Errors*. The two Dromio characters have to appear as the same identity to both the audience and to other characters in the play.

In creating the mirror image, one will find that it is the subtlest observations that work. The actor must pick up a rhythm, a certain cadence of a walk, or interpret how they hold their head. There is always a specific point of entry in catching the impression of another, that one little detail that, once mastered, informs the rest of the body, allowing for many other details to manifest themselves. Of course, the actors are helped by costumes and wigs to resemble each other, but the physicality is the key to success.

Being able to observe and then evoke the movement, rhythm and patterns of another actor is a basic exercise in character study. An understanding of the Alexander principle helps the actor to learn how the organization of coordination of another begins with the 'primary control' or the relationship of the head/neck/back. In a perfect world, the actor will learn how to play the tension of a character without taking on the tension in the body. If one can analyse how the tension or pressure in another body creates a shape affecting coordination, then with that awareness one can allow the shape into one's own body without setting the neck or tensing the muscles. Ideally, the actor creates the character without taking on its tension and is what we call 'good technique'. An actor cannot afford to play tension with tension, but must be clever and play a character's tension with intention.

Stage and film actor Colm Feore gives a practical and technical example of preparing the role of the famously eccentric pianist Glenn Gould for the film *Thirty-Two Short Films About Glenn Gould*. He describes his character process as 'imitation into evocation'.

When I came to play Glenn Gould for the film, the image, the shape I saw was a hedgehog at the piano. This character process began while I was in rep in Stratford, playing Mercutio and Berowne, so I could not keep that shape, except when I needed it. I was going to need it filming on a Tuesday and the next Friday and the following Thursday, but not in between. So I began by researching film footage and finding the shape of the man: how does he live? We know he took drugs, but he still survived. He played the piano brilliantly, almost seemingly from underneath the piano, with his back all croaked, his nuts in a twist, his legs crossed in a big pretzel, yet he was still breathing. You could tell he was still breathing fully, passionately; he was having a good time. In playing Glenn Gould, a famous modern personality that people know and have seen, I had to go from imitation to evocation but we had to pass through imitation to find a shape, to bust the limits of it, to break my habits and to find his habits and say 'OK, where does that take us?' It was a process of cut that, take that, reduce this, until finally I got to a place where I was just evoking a memory of the man.

5. The Kissing Class

Staging and performing a kiss in a play can be both a spatial and a physical problem. Working on kissing must be fun and playful so that the players can lay down their inhibitions or hang-ups and rehearse satisfactorily. For the actor, the partnership of every kissing dynamic is different and, of course, relative to the character and the story. How to sustain and heighten the tension and the anticipation of physical contact between two characters is created by the actors' bodies and physical energy. There are technical aspects to playing the kiss effectively. The audience is also involved in the dynamic. They have an insider/outsider's point of view on the excitement between the actors and therefore the sight line and spatial perspective has to be accessible and open to the audience. If the audience can see an energy exchange between the lovers, they will experience a palpable feeling of the excitement in a love scene. It is prurient, but it is entertaining.

I called a rehearsal with two actors to work with the kissing in a love scene. The problem was simple: he was 6' 4" and she was 5'6". The height differential made the kiss awkward. In the love scenes and when they kiss, it is important that actors see each other as well as the audience must see and feel the dynamic of the actors' intimacy. This can be achieved in an embrace if the actors give each other space between their bodies to allow for movement towards and away from each other. If they pull in too tightly and anchor the body at the pelvis, it restricts and limits the space in which the energy and the story between them can be exchanged.

I asked the partnership to each define their kinespherical diameter in space. With his tall height and the range of his arms, there could be a wide breadth of space between them in playing the first touch or physical contact. It was in the travel time of his hand and arm moving to touch her that the energy and intensity of the moment could be heightened. The exercise of moving in and out of each other's sphere and possible range of contact stimulated a creature awareness and heightened the chemistry between them. Both actors became more vulnerable and excited by the presence of the other. There was a delicate and intimate exchange between them. We all squirmed and giggled after they released the focus and attention on each other, a sure sign that they got the love story fired up.

We moved on to the technical problem of their height: that he had so far to bend over to kiss her. It was observed that he was collapsing in his neck and upper body and stretching his face forward and down in order to make contact with her. She, on the other hand, was reaching up with her chin and face towards him and contracting her head backwards in the process. The exchange was awkward, creating an unflattering picture. With a little attention to the Alexander Technique and some hands-on assistance from me, we worked out a solution. When he moved at the hip joint in opposition or away from her, engaging his lower-back muscles and releasing the knee and ankle joints in his legs, he could lower himself, at the same time freeing his head and neck to bend gracefully to give her his kiss. She, too, had to shift her pelvis back and away from him to allow the extension of her lower-back muscles to reach forward and up to receive the kiss; eliminating the contraction of her head and neck. In other words, they needed to create more space between their bodies in order to travel towards one another. If the bodies moved in too closely, they limited their room to move, which resulted in them contracting their necks and upper bodies in order to make contact.

The audience requires the extra room between the lovers to allow them in to see and sense the movement that creates the dynamic of the union. It is the approach and sustained anticipation of the lovers connecting with a kiss that excites the audience; watching the landed kiss and contact is not as interesting. Furthermore, it is more theatrical to experience the realization of the kiss which heightens as the actors pull away from one another and return to the autonomy of their physical space. The actress felt that by moving or shifting her weight back, she was able to see all of him in playing the moment. In realizing and seeing each other in space the moment after the kiss, the story kicked back in as they exchanged the chemistry of their dynamic.

The dramatics of staging a kiss lies in the question of whether the kiss is or is not going to happen. If there is a kiss, the drama heightens when the characters recognize the wonderment that they have kissed. Both actors felt that that the exercise was useful. They were able to take the work into rehearsal and apply it to scene work.

Many times I have had the amusing task of springing a 'kissing class' on a group of young actors. I never announce that we will be focusing on kissing; I simply keep my agenda hidden in spatial awareness partner work. I drop in the kissing challenge when I sense that the actors' spatial dynamics have been sufficiently heightened. Most actors are surprised but willing to kiss the acting partner, whatever their gender, after exploring the spatial dynamics of the partnership. For those who are not yet ready to make a plunge, the 'kiss of betrayal' on the cheek or the 'kiss of death' are options.

The actor playing the objective of seduction or aggression will be in a heightened physical state. It is the actor's intention and imagination that informs his body and thereby the audience can discern what the character is experiencing. Alexander's idea of the 'primary control' and a forward and upward direction in the organization of the body is very natural and evidently occurs in a emotionally heightened body. Suffice it to say, there is a stimulating yet fine line between seduction and aggression and both ideas are embodied in the actor's physicality.

6. Nudity

The issue of nudity on stage is always charged. Naturally, nudity is different for the male and the female. The male will feel exposed and vulnerable if his genitals are in full view. He will live in fear of any evident arousal. Whereas the female is more self-conscious and vulnerable when her breasts are exposed.

Being naked in the theatre, the actor is perceived at a distance, but the audience is live and their presence is palpable. Nudity is a big hurdle for the actor. The biggest hurdle, of course, is the first time they bare all. The manner in which this is handled in rehearsal requires some dialogue and sensitivity from the director, stage management, crew and fellow actors.

Once, while working with a young actress, I listened to her fears of the upcoming rehearsal where she would have to remove all her clothes for a production of *Equus*. After listening to her trepidation, I suggested that we both take our clothes off, right then and there. Here was Alexander's principle of inhibition in action, an opportunity to say 'no' to the fear and to step off into the unknown was the order of the day. So I simply began to remove my shirt and bra and stood before her in the rehearsal studio without a stitch on. Shocked and giggling, she jumped into the experience in a free and playful fashion and we ran about the room, airing our bodies to the elements, squealing like schoolgirls. This is not the usual fare for an Alexander class, but we addressed the problem that was blocking her freedom of movement and her exploration of character. The director of *Equus*, who was also a bit shy about how to initiate the nude scene, was delighted to learn that the ice had been broken and so the feared first rehearsal went along seamlessly. I received a well-deserved bottle of red wine.

Once the actor has been observed naked on stage, the audience quickly adjusts to the nudity, and the shock and curiosity is short-lived. I saw the actor Ian Holm as King Lear in the Cottesloe, the smallest theatre at the Royal National Theatre, where he chose to play the dramatic storm scene naked. His nudity actually heightened the character's battle with the onset of madness and nature's elements. Certainly, like any curious animal, I looked and observed his nakedness, but it was so appropriate for the storytelling that I was quickly drawn further into King Lear's experience of the storm.

When faced with the issue of nudity, the Alexander Technique can give the actor information to become self-aware or self-conscious of the body in a positive and constructive way. With regards to coping with nudity on stage, the actor must first step off and experience it. Then he can observe how the body responds. Does the breathing change? Does he contract the abdominal muscles to pull in the belly? Is the actor experiencing any tension in the neck and shoulders? What is happening in the feet and legs? Does the actor feel ill at ease? How is he seeing out in his world? Is there a tendency to look down at the floor, or is his vision more alert and peripheral? Does moving about free or restrict the actor? The response to all these questions and observations is information for the actor to begin making choices about what he wants to do or undo in the body as a result of nudity.

Alexander's concepts of 'inhibition' and 'non-doing' can be helpful tools for finding the suitable balance of tension with ease and naturalism. It gives the actor a mental edge and the means to tell the story without habits and physical hang-ups getting in the way of the character and the situation. The actor can begin to tell the body to release and let go of extraneous tension such as sucking in the stomach and tightening the legs. All of these choices are physical in nature and they must be rooted in the emotional life of the character.

7. Alexander with Costumes, Wigs and Period Accoutrements

Very often, actors come to me with technical movement problems related to dealing with costuming, wigs, hats and props. When we watch a film or a play set in a historical period other than our own, we identify the historical time and place according to elements of design. Some of these elements present a challenge for the actor. For example, the Restoration period requires huge powdered wigs for both men and women, corsets, high-heeled shoes, fans, capes and swords. These elements alone will create and demand a style for performing the period authentically.

The actor's body needs to adjust to and assimilate these exterior elements that can change the body's balance, breath, peripheral vision and spatial requirements on stage. The Alexander teacher can allay an actor's concerns about neck tension and back discomfort that may accompany the rehearsal process as the technical elements, staging and acting are added.

One actress recalls her experience of the physical challenges of playing different roles in repertoire:

> In the classical theatre, you have a lot of classical accessories or encumbrances. I found, working with the Alexander Technique, that those encumbrances could become enhancements if you adjusted to them and became aware of what they were doing to your body. For example, as soon as you don a corset, it does something to your body. Immediately, you breathe a different way. Often, when you have the corset on, you think you can relax everything and let the corset do the support work, but in fact you make it harder on your back if you are sinking into the corset. You must come up and out of it, letting the corset give support but not be a casket for your ribs. When you get up from a chair with a corset on, you have to think of leading with the head, otherwise it feels like moving furniture around. In the play *St Joan*, I was working with male accoutrements that I was not used to. I had a big broad sword, not a rapier or a foil. The weight and size of the broad sword was doing very strange things to my hips. I was adjusting by sitting into my hips and tightening my legs. Compensating by pulling back created a real stress point in my hips. So the Alexander teacher helped me see that I could come forward and up and out of my hip joints. I learned how to walk, sit and move with the sword, finding a way to move so that sword became an enhancement. I could sit and feel natural and comfortable with the sword because I was aware that I needed to adjust in my body to make allowances for it. My Alexander teacher made me aware that I was tightening in my upper back, jutting out my hips and supporting all my weight on my right leg and foot. 'Oh, there's that little pain in my back again, I'm cramping in my neck, my head is pulling back.' I was able to adjust by moving my head and body upwardly. The awareness lets you make a change. When I played Viola in the cavalier period, I

thought I would be freer to move as the boy Cesario, but it was not so, I had a sword, a breast-binder, high-waisted pants, a large hat and two-inch heels. It felt like my body was all chopped up and I was walking around arching my back. It was helpful to work with all the costume stuff with the Alexander teacher, who can see what you are doing in your body. The teacher can watch you specifically in rehearsal and see what is getting in your way and help you release the overarching in the back The awareness allows the problem to become part of your character rather than an irritation. The Alexander Technique is directional; it keeps you moving your energy upwardly, not down into the floor. You begin to move through the world on stage as a child does, with economy, ease and natural grace. When you are in repertory theatre you can be rehearsing in fourteenth-century Venice in the morning and then jump to roaring twenties Paris, all in a day's work. An actor might be playing a role in the 1920s or the 1930s with fashion problems like wearing four-inch heels and platforms on a raked stage. All these costume problems are thrown at you and your body has to cope or more than just cope: you have to be on top of it, as if it were not an issue. I recall wearing heavy robes in *King Lear*. I needed to appear as if I were born to wear that cape, without feeling that my shoulders were carrying the weight of the world. Alexander work helped me to engage the strength in my lower back by lengthening the spine as the supporting structure rather than collapsing all those muscles. It takes practice and technique to turn so that the cape turns with you and you don't jerk it around. With any huge piece of costuming, long trains or heavy capes, you have to move in it to see what it does to your body and how you can make it look good. You have to learn to let it be part of you and enhance the character with some consciousness of it.

Actors will often moan about the wigs and corsets.

There's the hair issue, with all the wigs. The fact that you are not wearing your own hair is for me a constant challenge to make it feel like it is your hair and your head with the hair. For example, the large hats I wore in My Fair Lady. Carrying off the size of the hat with a wig in between it and your real head was a big adjustment. The Alexander Technique idea of freeing the neck definitely helps you to feel less of the restriction. Wearing a corset is difficult because it is easy to become panicked when you go to breathe your normal way and you can't, so then you try to force the air in and you can't because the corset is restricting. It can be frightening. Alexander is helpful in that it allows me the choice of, well, if I can't breathe there, where can I breathe? I can breathe a little lower down, I can breathe higher up into my back, and that is a choice. I learned to enjoy the corset because I could sense my ribs moving and I could feel where the breath was active and supported in my body. There are so many unusual things in the theatre that get thrown at you. A musician sits at the piano, where she has been sitting since she was six years old, and, sure, the music might change, but she'll never suddenly wear a suit of armour or a funny hat while performing. Whereas in the theatre, there are all these weird things that you have to deal with, like wearing wigs and huge costumes, and the Alexander teacher helps the actor to integrate all the technical elements.

8. Mask Work

The key to exploring a mask is to begin in neutral, in order to allow the expression of the mask to come up and out through the body. Donning a mask, whether it be a neutral mask or an expressive mask, reveals much about the body of the bearer. The actor's own personal habits and tension in the body are heightened and dramatized by the mask. It can be comedic to observe how heightened the actor's physical habits will become by simply wearing a mask. A subtle or simple movement such as a shrug of the shoulders or a shift of weight on the legs will read much more dramatically if the actor is wearing a mask. The novice tends to allow too much movement and the mask work becomes too busy and erratic. Therefore it is very important to keep one's movement simple.

The actor needs to allow the mask to work its magic from within, to inform the exterior. When the actor can let go of the trying and controlling of the body and listen to and give over to the mask, then something unfamiliar and surprising can occur. Again, as with the Alexander Technique itself, it requires a willingness to explore the unfamiliar and let go of preconceived notions of how the experience should manifest itself. This process of trusting and allowing the body to have an unfamiliar physical and kinesthetic experience is a way of breaking habits and extending the body's range and expression.

An acting student stated:

> I loved the mask work. It was interesting, as I am such a facial actor. I remember in one class we spent a long time with the mask and I observed that when actors took the masks off, their faces were all relaxed and their eyes were huge and glistening. I became aware that there was a rosy-cheek kind of energy that was emanating from the whole body. We all try to express so much with our face, but with the mask you have to actually express it in the body. I was liberated by the mask as it allowed my body to express itself and not rely on my facial expression.

When experimenting with masks prior to using them in rehearsal, it I can be helpful for the actor to remember some of the information in the Alexander work with regard to thinking about the freedom in the head, neck and back. So much of human perception is processed in the head. All of our senses are housed in the head. Our organs for the senses of taste, smell, hearing and vision are in the skull. When the actor dons a mask, he might feel that his senses are interfered with or altered by the mask. Initially you will see the actor attempting to peer out of the eyeholes in the mask by contracting his head and neck. In an effort to see out, he will push his head forward into the mask. The audience will see the mask poking out as if detached from the body.

It is helpful for the actor to recognize the origin of vision. Technically, we do not see out of our eyeballs, as the optic nerve is located at the back of the head or skull. The origin of vision is from the back of the skull. When we restrict our vision when donning a mask, it is helpful to remember the origin of the vision, to allow ourselves to see out of the mask effortlessly. Relaxing and remembering how the origin of the vision is at the rear of the skull allows more freedom in the neck, enabling us to see out despite any blockage in the eyeholes of the mask. If the head is poised freely and easily on top of the spine, then the mask has more options and range. Freedom in the neck and spine of the actor enhances the movement of the mask and the mask will be integrated and married with the actor's body. An exercise to experiment with your perception follows.

Vision Exercise

● Lift one hand up and out in front of you.
● Observe your hand as if seeing from your eyeballs.
● Move your fingers and hand slowly about in space.
● Let your hand come down.
● This time, as you bring your hand up, think of seeing the hand from the optic nerve originating from the back of your head.
● Move your hand around in space, allowing yourself to observe the hand from further back in your head.
● Bring your hand down.
● Was there any change in your vision?
● Did you notice your peripheral vision coming into play?
● Were you seeing a broader, more open perspective of your hand as it moved through space?
● Did you sense a subtle response inside your head and neck? Was there movement at the occipital joint?
● Were your eyes more active? Perhaps we do have eyes in the back of our heads after all!

9. The Zoo Project – An Animal Study

Keen observation is a vital tool for an actor. To consider becoming and acting out the behaviour of another character is a multifaceted challenge that involves the body, the mind, the voice and the psyche of another spirit. It is a standard movement exercise at most drama schools around the world to do some sort of animal study.

The exercise I will describe is enhanced by access to a large zoo with a variety of species. The zoo allows the young actor to observe the animal in the flesh, despite its captivity. In this exercise, the actor is asked to make a choice from any of the varied species; one that is available for live observation at the zoo is preferred. It is interesting to see what animal the individual actor chooses. The actor is encouraged to observe the animal for several hours to see how the animal behaves, breathes, moves and sees out into the world. Once chosen, there are so many details about the animal to consider: the rhythm, the weight, the breath, the sex, the size and speed of the animal as it relates to its world of captivity. What are its basic needs? How, what and when does the animal eat and drink? Is it a social creature and how does it fit in to the social structure? Or is it a loner? How much space does the animal require and what environmental elements does it favour: warm or cold temperatures, trees to climb and swing in, water to play in, open space to roam? How does it cope and behave within captivity? All these questions are easily researched by the actor.

If the actor is familiar with the Alexander principle of the 'primary control', he will be able to study the organization of the muscular-skeletal system of the animal. Perceiving the 'primary control' is key to understanding how the animal moves and organizes its unique skeletal/muscular system. The head of the animal is always balanced in relationship to the spine. The freedom in the neck, as the head moves in a forward and upward direction, allows the spine to lenghten as the animal moves. A supported poise and readiness to move is what empowers the tiger as it watches its prey. The graceful ease and efficiency of the animal's movement is endlessly fascinating.

For example, the length of a cheetah's spine, the power and use of its tail, the connection of the tail to the movement and the power of the hip joints and the back legs are so apparent as it moves. As one walks about the zoo, one notes the largeness of the lion's head, the weight and power of the elephant's trunk, the seemingly human expressions of the chimpanzee, the relaxed movement of the camel's jaw, the rhythm of the sea otter, the head and neck extension of the meerkat, the staccato movement of the eyes and head of a parrot, the panting breath pattern of the wolf, to give just a few examples of the many unique details of every animal.

What is evident in all cases is the fundamental 'primary control' in action: the freedom in the neck as the head moves in a forward and upward direction allows the spine to lengthen as the animal moves.

Once the actor has chosen an animal and then observed it for an hour or two, it is ideal to have the actors meet in a space or studio provided by the zoo. The immediacy of going right into the studio allows an opportunity for the actor to apply his own body directly to explore the details observed in the chosen animal. We would begin the improvisational exercise with a few rules. For example, there was not to be any interactive animal behaviour other than seeing and observing one another in the space, as there would be conflicting species present. It was too early in the exploration of the animal to enact life-threatening defensive behaviour.

The actors initiated the exercise with a quiet entry into the animal, allowing time for their bodies to imagine the skeleton and the muscles of their creature. A sense of the animal's body structure and movement needs to come through the actor's own human form as if by osmosis. As the actor begins to get a sense of the weight, size, proportions, breath, rhythm and the primary control of the animal, the actor will embrace and embody the otherness of the animal. It is important not to rush the entry into the animal body as assimilating the small details of the animal gives the actor time to connect to the essence of the creature. It can be helpful to have the actors begin with a sleeping animal, in order to be in repose, to connect with the breath and size of the animal. Then gradually have the animal awaken and enter back into the environment in which it lives. As the creature sees out into the world, its eyes are in its head and the head/neck relationship will reveal something about the character of the animal. After our initial trip to the zoo, the next few weeks we devoted our time in movement class to the re-enactment and further study of the animals. The actors were encouraged to do more research and perhaps make a second trip back to visit the animal at the zoo.

As an Alexander teacher, I was able to help the actors with some hands-on direction and guidance to increase and heighten extension and flexion as they moved in the body of their animal. The challenge for the young actor to sustain concentration and the focus of being another creature for fifty minutes demands discipline and stamina. Since the actor exercises his entire body and asks muscles to create shapes and movement entirely foreign to his habitual use, this exercise stretches the range of movement and flexibility of the young trainee.

As the weekly exploration unfolded, the actors began to explore relationships with similar species: we began to see the chimpanzees swinging on the jungle gym, wolves moving in a pack, cats hissing to mark out territory, gorillas communicating by beating their chests and a variety of captivity behaviour developed. The sound or the voice of the animal came after the breathing and the rhythm of the animal was fully integrated. With each passing week, the animal study grew deeper and more authentically animal. The acting students were often amazed that forty minutes had passed, proving that time flies when your imagination is focused and absorbed into the body. When the imaginative and mental will of the actor is committed to the size, weight and energy of the animal, an observer would suspend disbelief and see a tiger or a warthog manifested in the rehearsal studio.

At one point, an invited audience came to the space to observe the animals, as if at a real zoo. To recreate the zoo we used a few studios and a gymnasium to separate the species in different areas or cages. After a good physical warm-up, the actors went to the makeshift cages and allowed the animal to enter the body. The audience was free to roam and to comment on the animals and some even tried to feed them, against the policy of the zoo. The actors were confronted for the first time with the temptation to entertain the audience and to lose concentration. For most of the young actors, it was the first presentation at theatre school and so the battle with nerves and excitement gave them the opportunity to use the Alexander training to direct their energy and go forward and upward into the work. Overall, it was a successful experiment in sustaining a focus and a commitment to the animal for the hour-long viewing. It was a wonderful exercise in 'less is more' and that 'acting is believing'.

One young actor described his experience with the animal study:

The value of the zoo exercise was immense. I chose a Chinese spotted leopard, a small cat, very long and sleek and skinny. I identified with it, physically. The whole experience of going out to the zoo and observing these beautiful creatures and letting one hit you with its presence was enthralling. I really wanted to learn how my animal moved and why it moved the way it did. My leopard was in a cage but moved everywhere in his cage and he did not stop. I remember the shoulder blades on the animal were in constant flow, never stopping, never any jerking movement. Everything moved: the head would move around, the legs were moving and the tail would respond with the movement of the body. I had a sense that my cat knew how to move, hunt and kill on an instinctual predatory level. When we went into the studio and started to work on our animals, it was just like getting into another skin of a character, it became a primal thing. Becoming the animal was the ultimate test in characterization: your body and your mind had to embrace the animal. I learned how I could move my shoulder blades the way the cat moved its shoulder blades and although I am a biped, I could still move and coordinate my joints and thigh muscles as my haunches. I do have a small tail and it is the power source of my back, yet my mind could image that tail bigger, extending like a wave of power. I imagined what the animal's senses were like. The face of my leopard, with its eyes set back deeper, engaged and expanded my peripheral vision. It was interesting to consider how the cat ears hear from up higher on your head, and so sound was coming in from a more forward and upward place. My awareness of the 'primary control' and the skeleton helped me to feel my skeletal structure change into the cat's. I remembered that the cat's neck was long and thick. He had large jaw muscles and a big neck to crush and kill his prey with immediacy. Sometimes I would start seeing spots because I was so into my cat. I was almost hyperventilating doing the cat's breathing. Eventually, I was able to mimic the cat voice and the way the cat breathed with a deep, low sound, leaving the mouth open. The process of learning about the character of that animal by using my mind and body as an expressive tool was one of the most enjoyable experiences I had at theatre school. I had no idea that I could imitate or become such a majestic creature. There I was on all fours on the ground, slinking, not walking but flowing, not stopping, constantly moving. My cat had a rhythm and everything moved to this clock in this animal that ticked. Time would pass so quickly as we were concentrating so intently that an hour would go by in a flash. It was a lot of fun.

A young actress, remembers:

The zoo exercise was so good for character work; the power of observation of specific details. The Alexander work helped me understand
where the animal's energy lies, where the animal sees out from with
an on-guard, 3-D awareness. In character work, you focus on intention, going for something and wanting something. That's what animals have; they don't have any pretence, they aren't masking
anything; they just are what they are going for. When you watch an
exciting actor, they are animalistic. You always know what he wants.

10. *The Lion King*

Having enjoyed the study of animal movement, I was delighted to be
called on board to participate in the mounting of the Toronto production of Julie Taymor's *The Lion King*. The production presents a variety of animals in masks, elaborate costumes and puppetry that are
marvellously theatrical and inventive. The show is wild, wonderful
and visually spectacular. It is a unique experience in the theatre.

The production management at Mirvish Productions in Toronto
hired a medical team with a chiropractor, physiotherapist, massage
therapist and myself to pro-actively take care of the cast, as they were
aware of the enormous physical demands of the show and the potential for injury. Considering the show would run for a year, perhaps
more, the producers saw the need for an animal husbandry team. The
cast was made up of dancers, singers and actors who played characters that were almost entirely animals: lions, hyenas, warthogs,
meerkats, cheetahs, giraffes, guinea fowl, zebras, baboons, birds,
wildebeests, rhinos and even elephants. Such a lavish array of
creatures presented many interesting physical challenges for the
human body.

It was my task to help the actors accomplish the various shapes and
challenges of playing such a wide spectrum of the animal kingdom. I
worked with the cast members throughout the rehearsal period. I rel-
ished analysing the movement and coordination issues that faced the
individual actors with each animal character.

Puppetry was an important element of the show. Some of the animal characters' costumes were life-size and some even larger than life. The comic warthog character, Pumbaa, was the size of a kitchen table, with the actor strapped into the centre with a large warthog face in front and the body and tail legs behind. The fittings and early adjustments to the puppet were focused on balancing the two sections on the actor as well as learning to operate the large mouthpiece of the puppet. It was a unique learning curve in the development of character, as the actors were first-time puppeteers and needed to adapt to the technical issues of the puppet en route to playing the character. It was important for the actor to keep his leg joints released, because if he locked his knees and ankles, the torso and tail end of the warthog would appear static and lifeless. Amusingly, every time the actor's shoulders moved, so would the big ears of the warthog. The actor needed to remain forward and open in his lower back to support the demanding action of his arms opening and closing the expressive mouthpiece of the warthog. The actor's body required freedom in order to have the supportive breath to sing within the size and restrictions of the puppet.

The designs of the puppets, by Julie Taymor and Michael Curry, are ingenious. Some of the puppets were attached to a metal breastplate and worn by the actor. The actor might also wear a wire attachment on his head to facilitate subtle movement in the bobbing headpiece of the animal. The comic meerkat character Timon was a five-foot-tall puppet attached in front of the actor in this manner. Throughout the rehearsal process, it was fascinating to observe how, when the actor was free and flexible in his body, it was immediately transferred into the animal energy of the puppet and the mask. In Alexander terms, the primary control of the actor's head and neck directly affects the primary control of the animal he is playing.

The numerous hyenas were an interesting movement challenge. The hyena masks were suspended by wires off a headpiece, so that any movement of the actors' heads would manipulate the mask. Having some knowledge of the Alexander Technique could help the actors with ease and freedom in the neck, which would reduce any neck strain and enhance the creature expression of the mask. The hyena body shape was bent over and used crutches like legs for support and mobility. The costume was the mane and the humped neck of a hyena, which unified with the mask; a clever design. The 'C' curvature was stressful on the body, especially for the singers, who needed an open passage for the voice and vocal support. It was important for them to think upwardly and allow the sacrum in the lower back to have some flexibility and mobility. The actors needed to build up the muscles in the body to sustain the hyena shape throughout the long rehearsal days.

The giraffes were yet another movement and balance issue. The actors moved across the stage on four stilts while sporting a long-necked headpiece. They had to sit on a ladder in order to place their feet in a boot-like strapping for the back legs/stilts of the giraffe. The front legs were longer stilts with an arm brace and handles to move and manipulate each of the legs. The initial experience of moving off the ladder at such a height is exhilarating. The body is on an upward angle and the legs are bent in the boot casing. The viewpoint of the actor and how he sees out as he moves affects his balance. An actor who, out of a natural tentativeness, looked down at the placing of one front leg after the other would miss the flow and easy momentum in the movement of all the legs in sequence. A simple note to look forward and out improved the actor's balance and stability.

The zebras were a wonderful design. The neck and head of the zebra fastened out from the actor's chest and torso. The front legs of the zebra were the actor's own legs, while the body and hind legs were attached to his back. The head or muzzle of the zebra was manoeuvred by a wired headband so that any movement of the actor's head evoked the primary control of the zebra. Even with the presence of the actor's body intersecting the body of the zebra, they became married, as one creature.

Working on *The Lion King* was a unique learning experience for me. The show is so original and theatrical that you cannot compare it to any other. I learned a good deal from teaching the actors and dancers the application of the Alexander principles to such an array of movement problems.

11. An Elizabethan Bear

A new play by Timothy Findlay, *Elizabeth Rex*, has Shakespeare and a troupe of actors meeting Queen Elizabeth I on the eve of Shakespeare's death, 23 April 1616. One character, Ned Lowenscraft, is renowned for playing all Shakespeare's female characters and he keeps a bear that he saved from the bear-baiting pits. The bear character is on stage during a good deal of the play, which required an actor with movement skills and the patience to be in a heat-producing bear suit for such a demanding length of time.

Prior to the first rehearsal, the young actor playing the bear had done a good deal of research and studied film footage of bears in the wild and in captivity. The wonderful props and costume departments had experience of making bear suits for previous productions of Shakespeare's *The Winter's Tale*, for the scene where the stage direction reads 'Exit, pursued by a bear'. The designers had thought through the problems of building a large headpiece that looked authentic and could be securely attached to the actor's head to allow for movement. The actor's vision was restricted, however; he needed to see out through the mouth and the muzzle of the bear's nose. The front paws were built up about eight inches, which helped reduce how far the actor needed to bend over to make contact with the floor.

I was concerned about the strain and contraction of the actor's neck when he was moving about on all four feet. It was very important for the actor to work on freeing his neck and keep the headpiece moving very subtly to maintain his flexibility and balance. While moving in a bear's lumbering rhythm, and in order to play the weight and largeness of the bear's limbs, the actor needed to emphasize the release and flexion in all the joints in his legs and to stretch and open the pelvic floor. The bear movement required training to build up the muscular strength and fitness in the muscles of the legs and pelvis. It was helpful to direct the spine upwards as the actor rolled over into the bear shape and to continue to think up through the 'C' curvature of the spine as he moved his limbs. Alexander's principle of 'primary control' is very helpful when playing an animal. We believed in the bear when the actor maintained some subtle movement in the head and neck; it gave the bear life, as if he was actively sensing and smelling with his big nose. Without this gentle movement in the head and neck, the bear would become static and lose credibility. When working with the understudy for the bear, it became clear that the actor needed to build up his stamina and flexibility incrementally in order to sustain the shape and energy of the animal and to adapt to the claustrophobic aspect of the costuming.

12. The Injured Actor

The demands of the theatre are physically rigorous and sometimes dangerous. Performing eight shows a week with all the staging demands of repertory theatre can take a toll. As the actor is human and vulnerable, inevitably injuries occur on stage and off. A season never goes by without some incident. An actor may trip on stage in a huge costume and twist an ankle, or fall off a bike on the way to the theatre, or, worse, fall off the stage in a blackout. The potential for mishaps is endless.

Often it is the Alexander teacher's job to help nurture the actor back to fitness after injury. The Alexander work can help the actor rethink some staging in order to cope with an injury. The hands-on assistance of the Alexander teacher may help the actor to adapt and perform certain movements or staging with less pressure on the injury. The actor may need to recruit other muscles in the body to compensate for the injured muscles or tendons. The actor needs to remain aware so as not to develop new habits of tension and pressure when compensating for the injury.

On one occasion, the leading actress playing the teacher, Annie Sullivan, in *The Miracle Worker* was injured during the first dress rehearsal. During the choreographed fight scene in the dining room with Helen Keller, she fell awkwardly, straight on to her shoulder instead of rolling with the fall. She had rehearsed this fight sequence many times. Perhaps she missed a beat, suffered fatigue or had a moment's lapse of concentration and – boom! – an accident. It can happen in a flash. She was rushed to hospital and X-rayed. There were no broken bones, but she had strained her ligaments. Her shoulder swelled up and turned every colour in the rainbow. The situation was compounded by the fact that the injured actress was also playing the lead in a musical and that show was in previews. For this actress, missing several shows was torture: every fibre to her core was in conflict.

She would rather eat nails then stay out at such a critical point in the rehearsal process. But wisely, she took the time to begin the healing process and avoided further injury from pushing through the pain.

I worked gingerly with her around the injured shoulder. Mostly I was able to help free up the lower back and neck that were affected by the fall. We had a constant dialogue about what was going on with her body. The choreographer helped her to modify and rework some of the lifts and one dramatic fall in the dance numbers in the musical. After an initial rest and de-traumatizing period, we met to begin some gentle table work. The Alexander work was good for appraising and encouraging the range of movement in the shoulder joint. We worked on equalizing the balance and use of all the muscles in her back and shoulders. It was important for her to engage her whole body, to move up out of her hips and to activate the lower back in order to compensate for the reduced mobility in her shoulders. The healing capacity in the highly tuned body of a dancer is remarkable. She knew her body well: when to ice it, when to rest and when to give it a whirl.

It was wonderful to see her back out there for the opening night, knowing all the hard work and spirit that was driving her performance. We worked together regularly throughout the season, which helped her maintain her body throughout this physically demanding repertoire. None the less, months later and with many shows under her belt, she is still nursing the injury. She knew that she owed her body an extended rest at the end of the season to finish the healing process properly.

I worked with an elderly actress who had survived a serious fall. We worked together throughout her healing process. She fell from the balcony of the Festival stage when wearing a mask as an apparition in – yet again – the first dress rehearsal of *Macbeth*. It is quite miraculous that she had the strength and the spirit to come back on stage to act again. She broke her shoulder blade and her clavicle and had serious concussion. I was a witness to this serious accident and the experience still haunts me.

It is important to state that live theatre can be dangerous and risky. Safety is a grave concern and must be prioritized over spectacle and deadlines. Actors will take risks out of generosity when feeling the pressure to get a show up and running for an opening night. It is folly to lose sight of human vulnerability.

Although her healing process was ongoing, it was that actress's mental attitude and energy, which was so devoid of negativity, that was so impressive. Her positive state of mind seemed to be a major factor in her healing. We tended to do table work, as it allowed her to relax and begin to release some of the holding and muscular tension acquired from the injury. When an injured body is in the healing process, it is important to allow the body to withhold and protect itself from startling or abrupt movement. The body knows its own healing course and it will recover at its own pace. The Alexander Technique is merely a gentle means of encouraging the body to free itself and regain confidence and flexibility. This process can take time, and every individual will heal at their own unique rate. It is critical to respect this and not to push or overstimulate the healing body.

13. Understudies

Let's face it, being an understudy is a thankless job. It is a learning opportunity that looms and hangs about waiting to spring on the actor at the drop of a hat. Consider the daunting task of playing Hamlet or Medea, and then think of the poor bugger who has to understudy the role. Imagine being at home in comfy sweatpants and sitting down to watch a video as the phone rings with the startling news that Hamlet has been hit with a bout of gastric flu.

Understudies go on frequently and for a multitude of reasons. The understudy will have to explore the depths of emotion and learn all the lines, the blocking and the fights solely through a process of osmosis. Often he plays another minor role in the play and will have merely observed the character's journey from the sidelines. There will be a line run and the stage manager or assistant director will take the understudies through the scene work of the play. Hopefully, they will have some stage time and a full understudy run on the stage with production elements of sound and lighting. The director rarely has the time to rehearse with an understudy. It is more often the voice coach, fight captain or Alexander coach who assists the actor in a private tutorial, working through the technical aspects of playing the role.

I have worked with several understudies in their physical preparation of Richard III, one of the most physically demanding characters. The shape and contractions of the body must emulate the choices and staging of the original player, yet the understudy has to discover and evolve his Richard III in his own body in order to safely and convincingly portray the character. The Alexander work is helpful for the actor in creating the shape of the character with a minimal amount of neck tension and muscle constriction. The Alexander teacher will have an insight into the process the principal Richard III went through to develop his physicality of the character. Input from the coaches and stage managers may be all an understudy has prior to the understudy run-through of the play. The stage manager, fight captain and voice and movement coaches are often called into an emergency rehearsal or warm-up to get an understudy ready to go on. This is a frequent high-energy and stress-filled situation. Everyone in the cast is wide-eyed and vigilant in order to support the poor actor as he is shot out of a cannon and into the play.

One season, in the musical *West Side Story*, there were two full-time understudies, the 'swings'. The 'swing' covers several of the roles and dance tracks of the leads and chorus members. They have the crazy-making task of mapping and reproducing the staging of several individual characters. In a physically demanding dance show like *West Side Story*, actors go in and out of the show on a regular basis. I have seen a swing go into the first act as a Shark and return in the second act as a Jet. Learning the choreography and then maintaining individual characters and movement tracks is a schizoid process. Being able to sustain a steadfast readiness to perform is demanding. An understanding of the Alexander Technique principle of 'end-gaining' can help the swing to stay open and ready for the immediacy of being 'on'. A successful swing needs to demonstrate the height of professionalism, as vulnerability and human folly feature largely in their working lives.

14. The Ageing Actor

It is a shocking discovery, in an ageing body, when one's feet ache, the lower back lacks suppleness, the teeth seem sensitive, an old shoulder injury comes back to haunt one and it take days to recover from a hangover. Moaning about ageing seems clichéd, until it happens to you. 'Move it or lose it' is a truthful adage. Regular exercise is essential for anybody. With ageing, we know that flexibility and strength are critical to maintain a lively, vigorous body. The Alexander Technique allows for an analysis of movement and examines the questions: what is the quality of the movement when one performs, and are we moving with awareness? The quality of movement, like mercy, is not strained.

Classical repertoire is filled with wonderful parts for older actors. Consider the demands of playing King Lear, Polonius or Hecuba for an aged body and voice. One must have energy and stamina to meet the demands of eight shows a week in the theatre.

While I was working on the table with a leading classical actor, he told me that his doctor had looked at his X-rays and felt that his hip joints were deteriorating and that he should consider having a hip replacement. This is a frightening and worrying diagnosis for a seventy-six-year-old while he is in the throws of rehearsing King Lear. (Needless to say, he will not be carrying a dead Cordelia on stage with 'Howl, howl, howl!' She will be represented by a dummy.) He says he is experiencing stiffness in the mornings and he feels that the relentless Canadian winter has kept him from the daily walking which he needs to keep in shape. There is the added pressure of how much time he would need to recover from the operation and there are plans and demands for him in upcoming seasons. He is a big, strong-bodied man and has terrific mental energy. It was interesting to hear his fears and I encouraged him to listen to his inner voice as only he can know how much discomfort is he willing to live with before surgery becomes essential. A few days later, having talked to the artistic director and to his family doctor, he decided to postpone having the operation until the end of the season, but that meant that the theatre would have to take him on the risky terms that he could at any time drop out if his condition became too painful and the operation necessary. I told him that I was available to do whatever maintenance he needed. I could help him with table work by giving his legs a direction to open and lengthen away from the hip joint. Supporting and cradling the weight of the legs is a good way to release the hip joint. I also gave his leg muscles a massaging stimulus. I was able to get length out of his middle back and neck. The Alexander Technique could not cure him of this serious condition, but it would certainly help his recovery from the inevitable hip replacement when the time came.

I have enjoyed my work with an eighty-eight-year-old actor. When we first met, he was a vigorous going concern and he was seventy-two! It has been my mission to have a filthy joke for him with every class, as it is good to elevate his pulse with a hearty chortle. I was delighted to notice when he returned to the theatre one year that he had improved his strength from the previous season. The shape of his neck where the spine comes into the head had been very recessive the previous year and it showed a marked improvement. I think that, at his age, one's body can have good years and bad. His doctor says his spine is completely compressed, but he reports that the work at the theatre helps to keep him going. I was able to use a surprisingly rigorous touch with the old guy. He had a good deal of fluid retention in his feet and so I stimulated his feet and his ankles, which were very swollen. I was not afraid to exert pressure in his neck and limbs to stimulate the muscles. He needed a bit of a massage and a firm contact. He always responded well to a release and lengthening through his mid-back or the thoracic spine. When my hands reached down his back to the insertion point of his neck muscles and I directed my hands upwards, there was always a dramatic lengthening response throughout the length of his torso. The knee joints in both his knees had been replaced within the last six years. He needs help and support of his legs in order to stretch his hamstrings and back muscles. He always sighed with pleasure when I took the weight of his leg and directed it up and away from the hip joint while still stretching his thighs towards his chest. The more he could articulate the movement and flexion of his legs in the hip sockets, the better he was at bending and lowering himself in and out of a chair.

An actress who is at an age that is difficult to conjecture describes the challenge of having to play elderly and feeble characters despite her hale and hearty body and soul. The Alexander Technique is a useful tool for the actor making contracted postures and enfeebled body types.

At this stage in my career, because of my age, I seem to get the roles of arthritic old ladies and people on their last legs. I am often playing a great deal of the physical limitations of the character. In exploring these characters, I will think about the quality of movement and let myself get free and then I let myself go into whatever configuration the role requires in terms of the physical limitation of playing an old character. I am presently in performance, playing a role where I am lying in bed almost the whole play, playing a woman who is dying. It has been physically problematic. I can find myself in that bed and observe myself pulled down and contracted in. I can think: 'Wait a minute', then I will be aware of what I am doing with myself and then consciously move up while in the process of thinking about the response to the other actor in the scene. When delivering my response, something entirely different can come out, in terms of the quality of what I was saying. It is as if it opens up my consciousness to what can be truthful. If I am pulled down and stuck, then I am not opening myself to all the stuff that is there inside me. If I am in a state of freedom and ease, then I have a sense that I am including everyone else. I can reach the back of the house because I am not closing off. And it is that wholeness of what is coming from me that gets lost when I close off. The wholeness of the character and me, because it is a combination of the two.

The Alexander Technique can be very useful for the elderly, as it teaches them to actively think about movement and encourages them to be attentive to how they are using the body despite the decreased flexibility and stiffness in their joints. When they can direct their movement with a bit of constructive thinking and attention to freedom in the neck and spine, they gain more confidence and control of their movement. The older actors all respond well to the gentle touch and helping hands of the Alexander teacher. Ageing and acting are not for wimps!

15. Falling and Fainting On Stage

Learning to fall safely on stage is useful. Most actors have had some stage-combat training. There are countless theatrical situations that require an actor to 'hit the deck' and collapse on a hard stage floor. Actors need a technique to survive various staging demands: taking a punch, fainting, tripping, farcical pratfalls, and general rough and tumble. The principle of thinking of an upward direction is essential for the actor as he releases his body to elevate and fly through space. The intention of going up gives the body more time to organize and organically find balance and freedom before impact with the floor. It's not unlike the drunk who falls down a staircase and blithely reels back up and carries on his merry way. Loose joints and muscular freedom save the drunkard's ass.

One actor describes his experience:

When playing the character of Oswald in *King Lear*, I needed to be tripped and thrown around on stage. It is difficult when you rehearse the show over and over again, as there is the danger of landing improperly on the joints. Knowledge of the Alexander Technique allows me to adjust myself while moving through space to use the cushioning parts of my body for a safe landing. Touch wood, I haven't bruised or hurt myself. Thinking of the forward motion, and an upward direction as opposed to driving yourself down on to the stage, really helps. It also looks dramatic because it heightens and sustains the movement which gives the audience more to see. It helps make the action more specific and makes me, the actor, feel safer.

In my very first season at Stratford, I taught an actress who was playing both Rosalind and Lady Macbeth in repertory. In both plays, the characters faint or swoon. During rehearsals, the actress was repeatedly fainting. She was beginning to feel uncomfortable in her right hip and shoulder from the way she was hitting the deck in each of her fainting spells. She came to the Alexander class with this complaint. We got out a tumbling mat to cushion the fall, as we needed to examine exactly what she was doing. I observed that she initiated her swoon by contracting her head backwards and that her body was clearly heading for the floor and hitting the mat with a thud. There was too much downward pressure in her body. My first instruction was to encourage her to stop initiating the movement with a contraction of her head. With my hands, I asked her to pay attention to sending her head in a forward and upward direction and also to allow her body to follow that upward idea as she released the joints in her legs to swoon. It was essential that her intention was for her body to go upwards, not downwards into the floor. The upward direction allowed her joints to open and her muscles to lengthen, releasing the downward pressure in her action. Having found a new lightness and freedom with the upward direction, the actress began gaily fainting all around the almost empty studio. Before I could stop her, she swooned and whacked her head on the only chair in the room! Horror of horrors, I'd killed the leading lady in her Alexander class! Well, perhaps we should say that the Alexander Technique was so enlightening that the actress saw stars.

16. Drunkenness

Playing drunk is full of pitfalls. Too often, it is simply overacted. The actor becomes too loose in his joints and muscles and therefore too sloppy in his movement and speech. If the actor observes an authentic drunk, it becomes clear that the person is striving to seem perfectly normal and composed. Often the speech pattern is more precise and specific than when sober.

Theatrically, the irony lies in the drunkard's effort to feign sobriety. To play inebriated, an actor cannot wing it by flailing about. He must be highly tuned and balanced in order to extend and heighten his range of movement to appear out of physical control. The roles of Stephano and Trinculo in *The Tempest* command several drunken scenes and physical high jinks. The Alexander thinking of an upward direction with openness and freedom in the joints will allow the actor to dramatize and intensify the limits of his equilibrium. The actor must create the physical comedy in the drunken scenes safely and purposefully to endure the long run of a show.

I worked with a young actress playing the wide-eyed innocent character of Honey in *Who's Afraid of Virginia Woolf*, a character who has to become increasingly inebriated over the duration of the play. The play was set on a raked stage, which compounded the problem of moving in a seemingly drunken and disordered fashion. We discovered that if she released the front of her ankles and allowed her feet to be playful with the distribution of her weight over the feet, she could adapt to the incline of the rake and maintain control of her balance. The contact with the floor and the release in her leg joints allowed for flexiblity and enough support for her upper body to allow her to play a collapse in the shoulders and loose weight in her arms. We had fun bouncing off the walls and the furniture to explore how far she could go off-centre and still maintain her balance.

17. Martial Arts and the Alexander Technique

The martial arts can be very beneficial training for the actor. All the martial arts focus on balance and centring the energy of the trainee. No matter what school of the martial arts, be it aikido, t'ai chi, karate, tae kwon do or judo, the student will learn how to stretch and enhance flexibility. The Eastern principle of yin and yang, representing the balance of the masculine and the feminine energy, in movement is a valuable concept for the actor, helping him to explore the spectrum of human nature. Martial arts heighten one's awareness of the lower centre. Tuning in to the energy source and power of one's centre is enormously helpful to the actor in terms of movement and voice. When the actor makes a real and truthful connection in acting, he is contacting his 'chi' or 'ki' in martial-arts terms.

The Alexander Technique is one method from Western culture that connects to a universal truth about movement and the body. Many cultures have discovered or explored movement in other forms. None of these forms or schools of movement are in conflict with each other and, when embraced, they can enhance the interdisciplinary under-standing of human potential.

I asked one trainee actor who came to the Alexander Technique classes with many years of karate training under his black belt, whether the Alexander work was helpful to him, and in what way. He responded:

Yes, with my karate, I had a system of movement in me already, an idea of alignment and specific techniques. I immediately tuned in to what you were saying about being free in your head and neck, although it was a different vocabulary and focus. I opened up to that different vocabulary and now I apply the Alexander Technique to karate almost all the time. As my awareness and understanding of the Alexander Technique grew, it propelled my karate training. I began to see in my karate world that someone could move beautifully in 'nikada', just like a dancer moving beautifully in a dance, but had not transferred that into how they walked, talked or the mental frame of mind they used to get on with themselves in the everyday. I had a class with this old t'ai chi master who was telling me 'Relax, relax' as he was moving my shoulders: 'No, no, soft, softer.' Just being told to relax doesn't help the relaxation, my 'sensei' or teacher did not have the tools to induce that freedom. But the 'hands-on' experience with the Alexander Technique teacher freed up my body in the moment which I could use to move. Now I can mentally draw upon it, I experience it as a mental remembering and then it allows my body to open itself. There is a mental process in movement, that when we think about it, something will happen. It's subtle, but there is a change. I think when you have a discipline like karate, you can apply the Alexander thinking and be able to read a subtle change because you are tuned in to the form of karate. Form is beneficial and repetition is a great teacher; the form is a point of reference. However, in my actor training, when I was walking or about to sing, in an effort to be grounded or centred, I would always take a martial stance, with my feet well apart. I had created a martial habit in my movement. Not unlike the habit of dance training, I carried my martial body into my regular body. The Alexander Technique gave me the awareness of how we use our bodies in various ways throughout the day. It gave me an awareness of what tension is and where it is in my body. I found new freedom within the form.

The Stage – How the Actor Adapts to Playing the Space

Where I work, at the Stratford Festival in Canada, we have three different theatres with three distinct types of stages, not unlike the Royal National Theatre in London, which has a thrust stage, proscenium-arch theatre and a smaller space in the round. Every theatre uniquely provides an opportunity for the actor to live in many different worlds. Consider the diversity of theatres, settings and productions that you have encountered. The actor needs to fill the space and conquer the venue wherever he tells the story. Every auditorium can have a mixed bag of virtues and drawbacks. The acoustics of the playhouse are contingent on architecture. Very often, it is the actor's job to overcome a bad acoustic with vocal training and technique.

The first day on stage in the theatre is full of significant information for the actor. The actor will assess the theatre, asking many questions. What kind of stage is it? How high is the proscenium arch? What is the depth of playable space on the stage? Is there an orchestra pit or a large apron frontage? How many seats are in the house? Is there a balcony or balconies? How far away is the furthest member of the audience? Are there sightline problems? Where does the actor naturally look when he sees out into the house? Is the floor of the stage raked? If the floor of the set is built on an angle, to what degree does it slope? How does the raked angle affect the actor's body and balance when he stands or moves about the stage? Does the actor lock his knees to counteract the pitch forward when standing still? Where are the exit and entrance ways? Does the set present any spatial or traffic problems? Does the set revolve? All of these questions will be addressed by the actor from a physical point of view. It is the body and the voice of the actor that adapts to the theatre venue. The Alexander work helps the actor to ponder and resolve the physical demands of playing and filling the theatrical space.

1. The Proscenium-arch Stage

Most nineteenth- and twentieth-century theatres are built with a proscenium-arch design with one, or perhaps two, balconies. The stage picture is framed. The open space is sometimes referred to as the 'fourth wall'. As an audience member, you can feel left out of the play when the actors fail to look up and out to include you. It is boring to view only the top of the actor's head and miss out on the expression of their eyes. For the actor to play a large playhouse, he must increase his peripheral awareness. The head and neck should be freely poised at the top of the spine to move easily and naturally, in order to communicate with the perimeter of the audience.

An actor's spatial attention may be referred to as 'working the house' and the good ones can do that on every variety of stage. Actors have a tendency to think in a frontal manner and physically push their faces and bodies forwardly as a means to break through the framing of the proscenium-arch theatre. The Alexander work helps to heighten the actor's awareness of the primary control in his head and neck as well as the full circumference of the body. By asking the actor to pay more attention to the volume and dimension of his whole back, he will fill the stage with his presence. When the actor moves up and off his hip joints, he will maintain more ease and agility on stage.

2. The Raked Stage

In the proscenium-arch houses, often the production will use a raked stage as a means to visually lift the show up. The raised floor may not be perceivable to the audience, but the actors feel it. Depending on the degree of the angle, it is comparable to wearing a high-heeled shoe. Often the actor has to wear a high-heeled shoe on the raked stage, increasing the grade of the angle and seriously affecting the organization of the body and balance. I stepped out on to the stage for the musical *Miss Saigon* and I was shocked by the extremity of the angle. Many of those dancers and singers suffered vocal problems and physical ailments over the long run of that show.

As an Alexander teacher, I have dealt with many complaints from actors coping with the effects of a raked stage. Most actors counter-balance the rake by leaning back, putting pressure on the lower back. They tend to lock the knees and settle into the hip joints as a device to anchor themselves. Locking the knees will hyper-extend the calf muscles and set the pelvic bone, thereby constricting the hip joints. All this locking-up in the lower body creates a condition that restricts breath and vocal support. Of course, one can still move but the subtle angle pitching the actor forward can wreak havoc on his bones and muscles.

Actors require technique and a constant attentiveness to how their bodies are adapting to the rake. They must think upwardly and go along with the forward inclination. Compensating by leaning back only gives the actor a false sense of security and produces pressure and tension in the lower back. As an actor moves back and upstage, the angle of the rake will increase. As he progresses upstage, he ought to move with a forward and upward direction, as if climbing a hill, to reduce the effort and downward pressure in the body. When standing in profile, an actor needs to come up and off the downstage hip joint, avoiding a downward contraction in that leg and allowing for quick and ready movement. All the Alexander principles covered in Part 1 are applicable to the technical difficulties of the raked stage.

3. The Thrust Stage

The thrust stage presents the play and the players out into the audience. At times the audience may only view the actor's back. The actor will sense the presence of the audience behind him and he will organically think more voluminously in his body. A thrust stage encourages blocking on the diagonal, and circular movement helps the viewer see the interaction of the characters. With a thrust stage, you will see the show from a different perspective if you sit on the other side of the house.

A widely experienced stage and film actor offers his thoughts on spatial awareness and the Alexander Technique when acting on a thrust stage:

> In order to be heard on the thrust stage, one needs to send a signal, in an Alexander way, to think three-dimensionally about the acting. The thrust stage, once mastered, offers the most realistic possibilities for acting: the most naturalistic, in the sense that it is completely three-dimensional. You leave your dressing room and you are out there, someone is seeing you from all around, so, consequently, your intention as that character has to be radiant and coming out from all the areas of your body. For me, there then comes this thrilling electric energy that zings around you when you define your space. Depending on what is going on in the scene, you tell people where they are because it is in relationship to where you are.

The Alexander Technique heightens the actor's awareness of the poise of the head on the spine, the volume of the whole body and the extension of the limbs needed to fill the expanse of a thrust-stage theatre.

4. Theatre In the Round

Theatre in the round presents similar demands to the thrust stage. The audience in the round encircles the playing space of the actor and therefore the actor must fill the stage voluminously and three-dimensionally. Often the seats of the audience are raked steeply upwards and around the stage. The actor is challenged to look upwards and out without over-contracting his head and neck in the process of acting in the round. Any over-contraction of the head and neck can create a pressure on vocal mechanism, causing potential vocal strain.

In Part 3, we discussed the importance of the primary control and freedom in the head and neck in voice production. Acting on a stage in the round is a prime time for engaging one's Alexander Technique to play the house with freedom and presence. The actor will need to up and open in the body to make a connection with the audience encircling him. Technically, the slightest movement of the head, engagement of the peripheral vision or a subtle shift in an actor's weight on the stage can make the actor more visibly available to the audience in the round.

5. Outdoor Theatre

Theatre outdoors has its liberating aspects and its drawbacks. The actor will immediately feel the vulnerability of being in an uncontrolled space, subject to natural disasters, the weather and free, roving public audience. The actor will naturally try to overcompensate for the big sky and start to push both physically and vocally. He must be vigilant about not straining vocally to reach his outdoor audience.

Training in the Alexander Technique will help the actor to identify when he begins to strain and over-extend himself through physical tension. The actor must elevate his vocal and physical energy to rise to the outdoor theatre experience, but it is vital that he should know when he is pushing his body past its range and limits.

Every style of stage and each theatrical venue uniquely presents new problems and issues in performance. The actor needs to step out into every new theatre, spend time in the space and assess its problems. You need to have the organic experience of speaking out into the space in order to get a kinesthetic feel for the stage and the auditorium and to assess the acoustic qualities of the venue. It is vital for actors to familiarize themselves with the stage and feel at home out there in the space, as one day the theatre will fill and they will be inviting the audience into the story.

Epilogue

My objective in writing this book has been to inform the reader of the importance and versatility of the Alexander Technique as it relates to the actor in theatre or film. I hope the reader has gained some insight into the training requirements and diversity of the actor's discipline and craft. An actor goes through a great deal of work prior to stepping out into the limelight and excitement of a performance. I hope this book inspires and encourages young actors to attempt novel and untried experiences. I often say to students, 'Hey, you can always come back to a bad habit.' The Alexander philosphy is that freedom lies in one's awareness that one can choose.

One young actor expressed how the Alexander Technique had become part of his approach to acting:

> Alexander Technique is, for me, a means to allow my body to empty itself of habitual movement or body traits and just approach character work from a neutral or fresh place; to allow the character work to amalgamate into that fresh body. It has kept me aware of what was where: where my head was; where my arms were; how my shoulders were placed; whether I was back on my hips or forward in my hips; were my knees bent? Knees straight? Whether I was tense. Before the Alexander work, I never would have thought of these questions as character choices. Now my world is more opened up to the physical. I am able to control subtleties that make the experience of acting a character more real. Hopefully the performance has become stronger and a little more convincing for myself and for my audience.

Mastering the actor's craft is an ongoing struggle and adventurous process. The actor constantly challenges his psyche to explore the unknown. Drama is riddled with tension. It is the actor's job to experience the stories emotionally and therefore physically. Actors should welcome any technique or tools that release and free up their bodies from the tension and demands of the theatre. The Alexander Technique is just one of many valid disciplines an actor may select to help him along the way to transformation.

Again, I must emphasize that the actor cannot learn the Alexander Technique from a book. One can experiment with exercises and learn about the concepts and principles of Alexander work, but at some point it is absolutely necessary to engage with a trained Alexander teacher in order to realize the benefits of the Alexander Technique fully.

I am confident that the Alexander Technique has a sound and valuable application to any actor training or ongoing professional work. I hope that this book will stimulate other Alexander Technique teachers to become involved with the creative process of acting. The application and adaptation of Alexander principles to an actor's physical problems is boundless. Perhaps other Alexander teachers will take up the gauntlet and use this book for guidance in exploring future work with actors.

In writing this book, I have reviewed my twenty years of teaching and learning within the world of the actor. I have so many artists to thank for letting me be privy to their conception and intimate imaginings of creating a character. It has been a privilege and a wonderful ride, to sail alongside the actors and their work.

This book has been focused on the demands of the theatre and the specific needs of the actor. Not everyone comes to Alexander work with an agenda to enhance performance. Some come for therapeutic reasons. I promise that any person who pursues Alexander Technique lessons will learn something about themselves which will change their life.

Addresses

I have listed contact addresses and web sites of international societies for Alexander Technique teachers below, to help the reader locate a teacher in their own region.

American Society for the Alexander Technique
AMSTAT
PO Box 60008
Florence
MA 01062
USA
www.alexandertech.com

Australian Society of Teachers of the Alexander Technique,
AUSTAT
PO Box 716
Darlinghurst
Sydney
NSW 2010
AUSTRALIA
tfitzgerald@ozemail.com.au

Canadian Society of Teachers of the Alexander Technique
CANSTAT
465 Wilson Avenue
Toronto, Ontario
M3H 1T9
CANADA
www.canstat.ca

Society of Teachers of the Alexander Technique
STAT
129 Camden Mews
London
NW1 9AH
UNITED KINGDOM
www.stat.org.uk

Alexander Technique International
ATI
World Wide Professional Organization for the F. M. Alexander
  Technique
Jan Baty, Corresponding Secretary
1692 Massachusetts Avenue, 3rd Floor
Cambridge
MA 02138
USA
www.usa@ati-net.com